BEINGNESS

Change Your State
of Being to Reprogram
Your Reality

Renee Minchin

BEINGNESS
Change Your State of Being
To Reprogram Your Reality

First published in Australia by Conscious Bias 2025
Books That Rewire
www.reneeminchin.com

Copyright © Renee Minchin 2025
All Rights Reserved

A catalogue record for this
book is available from the
National Library of Australia

ISBN: 978-1-7641133-2-8 (pbk)
ISBN: 978-1-7641133-3-5 (ebk)

Typesetting and design by Publicious Book Publishing
Published in collaboration with Publicious Book Publishing
www.publicious.com.au

No part of this book may be reproduced in any form, by photocopying or by any electronic or mechanical means, including information storage or retrieval systems, without permission in writing from both the copyright owner and the publisher of this book.

Contents

Introduction i

Part 1: Subconscious Programming

Chapter 1:   Creation Starts in the Mind 1

Chapter 2:   Programming and The Subconscious Mind 6

Chapter 3:   Understanding the Programming of
Your Environment 19

Part 2: Changing Your Perception

Chapter 4:   Reinforcing Your Reality
Through Perception 39

Chapter 5:   The Perception of Mayhem –
Redefining Chaos 50

Chapter 6:   Being "In Communication" 56

Chapter 7:   Decluttering the Mind 67

Chapter 8:   Removing Right and Wrong 72

Part 3: Pulling Forward Your Reality

Chapter 9:   The Creation and Loss of Identity 79

Chapter 10: Being Your Word 86

Chapter 11: Belief and The Purpose of Practice 93

Chapter 12: The Journey of Surrender, Letting Go, and
               Embracing The Unknown 99
Chapter 13: The Role of Gratitude................................ 105
Chapter 14: Standing In Your Power – From Being
               Influenced to Influencing 109
Chapter 15: Trusting The Network and Meeting
               God Matter... 113
Chapter 16: Masculinity, Femininity, and How
               They Intertwine... 118
Chapter 17: Breathwork, Trauma Lines,
               and Connectedness...................................... 128

Part 4: Creating Your Desired Reality

Chapter 18: What You Really Want (And It's Not What
               You Think!) – Depths of Realisation 137
Chapter 19: Power of Intention and Focus 143
Chapter 20: Letting Go of Attachment 150
Chapter 21: Bringing Into Being Through Action 156
Chapter 22: Mastering the Art of Being 162

Conclusion.. 171

Introduction

This book is about my journey with beingness. If we break down the Latin root of the word "being", the Latin verb *esse* means "to be", and from this, we get words like "essential", pointing to what is fundamental or necessary. "Being" is the essence of existence, but it's more than just occupying space or time – it's about consciously choosing. In the context of this book, being is the same as embodying a vibrational frequency. Being is about how you align with what you want to create in your life, about achieving your desires, and how you can take steps to allow those desires to be created in the physical world.

At every moment we are vibrating at a particular frequency, and this frequency is what shapes our experience of reality. Being means tuning in to that frequency – whether it's the frequency of love, forgiveness, anger, or creativity. We have the ability to choose what we are being in any moment. This connects to the theme of duality the idea that at any moment, we can choose between reacting (living unconsciously, out of habit) or creating (consciously shaping our reality).

I wrote this book because I felt a deep calling to share the experiences that have shaped my life, who I am, and who I am consciously creating myself to become. This book is more than just a reflection of my journey; it's an exploration of the realisations and transformations that have defined my path.

I've learned that life isn't about arriving at a fixed identity; it's about continually choosing who you wish to be and choosing in each moment, then lifting vibrationally to evolve into who you choose to be moment by moment, until you no longer choose. For this realisation, I want to express my gratitude to all my teachers: those who have entered my life, and those who are still to come – I look forward to meeting you. Each and every teacher has influenced me and shaped how I see myself, whether visibly or subtly. Each interaction has expanded or influenced me to discover my truth and gifted me a knowing where I can choose to step into who I choose to be.

My hope is for you to realise the immense power you hold to create whatever you desire. It all starts with a single step: *realisation*. When you understand that reaction is within your control, you gain the ability to create your life in any way that you choose. Life is an extraordinary gift, filled with limitless potential. The moment you recognise that the power to shape your reality lies entirely with you, possibility becomes endless.

This is what I would love you to consider: your reality is yours to create. You are both the creator and the created, and once you embrace that knowing, the life you want is well within your reach.

I also want you to understand that there's a subtle but profound difference between *being* and [to] *be*. Though simple, they are deeply connected. For me, *being* is a vibrational feeling – an individual realisation of spirit, and an undertone that resonates through every action, thought, and thing. *To be*, however, is to exist and take place.

This book is my exploration of the journey from simply existing to *being*.

Part 1

Subconscious Programming

1
Creation Starts in the Mind

Creation begins with an idea, a thought, or a concept. What's fascinating is that in order to create something, we must first be aware that it's possible. This awareness is key, because if we don't know that something can exist, how can we bring it into reality? Awareness might come from seeing someone else achieve something, reading about it, or simply envisioning it in our mind's eye. The first step is always awareness: we must know that it can be created before we can create it.

What's even more intriguing, though, is that sometimes we may not know the full scope of what we're creating at the beginning. The natural flow of energy reveals the next steps to us as we progress. It's as though creation unfolds in real time. You start with what you want and, as you move forward, the next step becomes clear. This is the beauty of the creative process – that the mystery and excitement lie in the unfolding, step by step. This is also why you cannot necessarily connect the dots going forward, but looking back you can understand why things evolved the way they did.

I've thought a lot about this concept of gradually unlocking the process – particularly during my travels, when I began to ponder the idea of happiness in different contexts. I often encountered people living in lower economic circumstances who seemed more content and joyful than those in so-called "wealthier" societies. You regularly hear remarks like, "They have so little, yet they are so happy". But I wonder: is their happiness rooted in a lack of comparison? Could it be that without a constant point of reference for what they have, they feel more content? What happens when a comparison point is introduced? When someone becomes aware of what else is possible – more wealth, comfort, or opportunities – does it then breed discontent?

This ties directly into the concept of creation. As we become aware of more possibilities, we open ourselves to new creations. However, it can also introduce dissatisfaction with what we currently have. The key lies in how we manage this awareness. Do we use it to inspire growth and action, or do we let it cause frustration and longing? Comparison can be a double-edged sword, but when understood properly, it becomes a guide rather than a source of discontent.

This brings us back to the core idea: creation must be embodied at some level, felt or seen in our consciousness before we can create it in reality. From that space of awareness, we begin the process of creation, bringing what was once intangible into physical form. This is where the magic happens. We create ideas and realities that might not have been part of our past experiences but somehow, through cultural or environmental influences, or simply through our inner knowing, we are able to create them.

But where do these ideas come from? Sometimes, they feel like they are born out of our personal experiences, but they can also come from something greater – divine inspiration, source energy, god matter, or the collective consciousness. In many spiritual traditions, this divine inspiration is seen as the true source of all creativity. We are simply vessels through which these ideas flow. We are co-creators with the universe, constantly interacting with energies, ideas, and forces greater than ourselves. As we tune into these forces, we receive inspiration. And as we act on them, we influence and uncover new realities.

Divine inspiration further ties into how we bring subconscious beliefs into the physical world. Our belief systems, which are often shaped by subconscious programming, dictate what we think is possible and what we create. I know that in my early years, I didn't fully understand the power of creation because I was influenced by the belief systems instilled in me by my environment. I was raised to believe that material success equated to achievement. I thought wealth and status were the ultimate goals, but as I grew older, I began to question whether these were truly my desires or simply the programming I had inherited from my upbringing.

We talk a lot about inner knowing – about listening to that quiet voice inside that guides us towards our true purpose. But even that voice can be influenced by external programming. How much of what we believe is truly our own, and how much of it comes from the ideas and values we've absorbed from our culture, family, and society?

Some spiritual traditions suggest that we choose our parents before birth, selecting the perfect environment to step into for the lessons we need to learn in this lifetime. While I'm not entirely sure if I believe this, I do know that the parents I had were exactly the ones I needed. How could they not be? Their vibrational frequency aligned with mine in some ways but not in others, and the lessons I learned from them shaped me in profound ways. However, I also think if everything we experience is patterning, it means I am nothing but the perception of myself as a reflection around me.

In the upcoming chapters, we'll explore how these belief systems are formed through our upbringing, culture, and subconscious programming, and how we can reprogram them to align with our true desires and the reality we want to create.

We'll also explore the interplay between masculine and feminine energies – how the feminine energy brings in the creative ideas, while the masculine energy provides the structure to manifest them. Creation always starts in the mind, but it is the balance between the flow of ideas (feminine energy) and the structure and action (masculine energy) that allows those ideas to become reality. When both energies are in harmony, creation moves seamlessly from thought through to creation. Throughout this book, we'll explore how this balance plays out in different aspects of life – how we can move from being influenced to becoming the influencer, how we trust in the interconnectedness of everything, and how masculine and feminine energies intertwine to bring forth the life we want to create.

Ultimately, the creation process is deeply personal, yet universal. It's about tapping into our inner knowing while remaining open to the divine source for all inspiration. We are uniquely ourselves, yet we are part of something far greater, connected to a web of energies, ideas, and possibilities. Creation is a journey and, as we walk this path, we realise that we are both the creators and the creation.

2
Programming and The Subconscious Mind

Whilst it is true that creation is something that starts in the mind, beingness and shaping the state of our reality are both also concepts that are core to the theme of this book. Before we can truly start understanding what beingness is and how we can shape our current reality into one guided by a state of being, though, it is important that we start off by understanding the fundamentals that have shaped what our current reality actually looks like. There are two main fundamentals that we are going to be looking at in this chapter: programming and the subconscious mind.

What is programming and the subconscious mind?

As you may already be aware, the conscious mind is the part that handles our active thoughts and immediate awareness. That said, when we talk about the subconscious mind, we are referring to the part of our mind that operates in the background, below the level of conscious awareness. Although we are not always fully aware of this part of our mind and the way in which it is working, the subconscious mind is home to a lot of information, habits, and ingrained patterns that shape our identity and how we engage with the world. Because of this, even though it is not something that we are really aware of a lot of the time, it still plays a big role in shaping our thoughts, feelings, behaviours, beliefs, experiences, and memories. It also influences the decisions that we make and how we react in different situations.

On the other hand, programming refers to the ways in which the beliefs, habits, and automatic responses found in our subconscious minds are shaped and influenced over time. Effectively, the experiences that we have and the information we are exposed to within our conscious minds will then go on to shape or program our subconscious mind and the subsequent behaviours, perceptions, and responses that result.

Just as computer programming involves programming or inputting data into a computer system, programming involves our subconscious mind absorbing information that we are exposed to throughout our everyday lives. This might be through certain experiences that we have (such as in childhood), the interactions we have with others, the information that we are told throughout our lives, and the things we tell ourselves. Our subconscious mind will then develop certain habits or automatic responses that are triggered based on these beliefs and patterns that become ingrained within our minds. For example, you may have been programmed to feel anxious when seeing dogs in public spaces, because you have always been told that dogs are vicious and scary. You may find that this fear ends up appearing automatically, even though you have not had any first-hand experience with a vicious dog.

The unfortunate reality is that, a lot of the time, the programming that our subconscious mind has been exposed to throughout our life can result in less than desirable automatic responses – be they sadness, anxiety, anger, self-doubt, or the good old fashioned "imposter syndrome". The good news is, though, that just as a computer can be reprogrammed and updated, we can also reprogram our subconscious minds to create new, healthier, and more positive patterns. Rather than our subconscious minds running on negative programming that plants seeds of self-doubt and avoidance, we can shift beliefs or habits into more empowering ones, and create new pathways within our subconscious minds that align better with our conscious goals.

Although much of the programming we are exposed to takes place within our subconscious minds, it can also take place within our environments and the beliefs we are exposed to and develop in different settings. This is something we will be exploring in more detail in the next chapter. For now, I wanted to talk to you a bit about some of my own experiences with programming and the subconscious mind.

Programming and the subconscious mind in childhood

This process of reprogramming and reframing thoughts is something that I have spent a lot of time working to understand my own journey to achieving personal growth and a better sense of overall wellbeing. This has required me to think deeply about my own programming and subconscious mind, including my experience of life and why it is that I am programmed in the way that I am.

For me, a lot of it can be traced back to my childhood. The subconscious mind, especially in childhood, absorbs its environment. The thought patterns we inherit from our family and environment often become ingrained in our subconscious, and this shapes our reality in ways we don't even realise. Frequently, these thought patterns continue to reappear as patterns throughout our life and continue to influence the way we see ourselves, others, and the world around us. It is only really when we dig deep and reflect on this programming that traces all the way back to our childhood that we truly start to realise from where many of these subconscious beliefs that we now hold have originated.

Spirituality and religion

My home environment had a profound influence on shaping my worldview, especially regarding spiritual matters. My father, although not traditionally religious, had a significant impact on my early programming around spirituality. He was deeply spiritual and spent many years experimenting with different religions, trying to find the right path that resonated with his understanding of the world. This spiritual exploration created a unique dynamic in our household – one that was both structured and open, depending on the phase of his spiritual journey.

My sister, who is much older than I am, frequently jokes about the inconsistencies she experienced during her childhood. She recalls how, on some Saturdays, she was allowed to play one week, then another week on the same day she wasn't, as Dad had changed religions. There were also some times where she wasn't allowed to engage in certain activities, depending on which religious practice my father was exploring at the time. These shifting rules were part of his journey to determine what felt right to him, and she bore the brunt of that enquiry.

By the time I came along, my father had moved beyond these fixed religious practices and adopted a more fluid spiritual approach. His spiritual journey had evolved from one defined by rigid religious rules to a more open and exploratory understanding of the divine. This openness to different ideas and concepts became a hallmark of my upbringing. I was raised in an environment where questioning, exploring, and thinking critically about spiritual matters were encouraged. Spiritual exploration and experiences were accepted and nurtured a connectedness between my father and me.

One of the key distinctions that became evident to me growing up in this environment, is the difference between religion and spirituality. Religion, from my perspective, is very rules-based and sometimes inflexible. It has clearly defined structures, dogmas, and practices to which followers are expected to adhere. Religion sets fixed boundaries for what is considered "right" and "wrong", and often operates within a framework of moral and ethical absolutes. Spirituality, on the other hand, offers more freedom. It is fluid and expansive, allowing for personal interpretation and for individual paths to be followed. My father embodied this fluidity in his later years, moving away from strict religious practices and embracing a more spiritual way of life that allowed for greater personal exploration.

This difference between religion and spirituality became extremely clear to me when I travelled to India. There,

I witnessed spiritual practices that were deeply rooted in tradition, yet they seemed to carry a different energy than the rigid religious structures I had seen before. I witnessed these people engage in repeated spiritual practices – rituals that, while structured, had a fluidity and flow to them. These practices weren't about enforcing a rigid belief system; instead, they were about building belief through repetition, creating a deep connection to something greater through continuous practice. This experience reinforced my belief that spirituality is about building belief through consistent practice. However, the key difference I see between religion and spiritual practices is that spirituality allows for more fluidity in how belief is built. It's not about adhering to a fixed set of rules, but about connecting to something larger in a way that feels authentic and personal.

Whilst the environment I grew up in was spiritually rich, it also had its limitations. My father, for all his openness to different spiritual ideas, still had certain fixed views. While there was always room for discussion and exploration, there were boundaries too, and his spiritual beliefs often carried with them their own kind of structure and dogma. These fixed beliefs created certain constraints on my own spiritual development, especially in childhood, where I began to internalise some of the rigid thought patterns he held and felt I could not express or enquire openly about all the time, especially if my experience or perception were different to his.

This meant that while I was encouraged to think critically and explore spiritual ideas, I was also influenced by the underlying structure of my father's beliefs. So, these subconscious patterns became a kind of programming that shaped how I viewed the world. For a long time, I accepted this structure without question, believing that spirituality had to fit within certain constructs.

As I've grown older, I've come to see that this spiritual programming was both a gift and a limitation. The openness my father fostered allowed me to explore a variety of spiritual concepts without fear of judgement. But his fixed ideas also created a rigidity in my thinking, or a belief that certain things had to be a certain way. This kind of rigid thought pattern is a manifestation of masculine energy – structured, linear, and often inflexible.

It wasn't until later in life, particularly during my time in India, that I began to understand the importance of fluidity in spirituality. When we become too rigid in our beliefs – whether spiritual or otherwise – we limit what can show up in our lives. We trap ourselves in fixed thought patterns and end up repeating the same actions, yet expect new results.

However, when we embrace more fluidity and allow flexibility in our spiritual practices and beliefs, we open ourselves up to new possibilities. This is where feminine energy comes in. The feminine is not about rigid structure; it is about flow, intuition, and adaptability. Feminine energy provides space for things to show up in unexpected ways. It is less concerned with controlling outcomes, and more focused on trusting the process.

By stepping into a more fluid approach to spirituality – one that integrates the feminine energy of flow – I've been able to release many of the rigid thought patterns that were programmed into me in childhood. This shift has allowed for new experiences, new insights, and a deeper connection to my inner self. It has shown me that spirituality doesn't have to be fixed or defined by rigid structures; it can be a dynamic, ever-evolving process that adapts to life.

As I began to break free from these fixed thought patterns, I realised that spirituality can be much more fluid. By embracing both the masculine energy of structure and the feminine energy of flow, I've been able to create a more balanced and holistic approach to my spiritual practice. This has allowed me to let go of the belief that things have to show up in a certain form, and instead, trust in god matter and know that the universe will bring what is meant for me in its own time, in its own way, and when I am ready. Now, to me, spirituality is no longer about following a rigid path, but about trusting the flow of life and the guidance that comes from within.

Formation and loss of identity

As mentioned, my father has had an enormous impact on shaping my spiritual journey and my sense of self. He fostered an environment where I was free to explore my spirituality, unrestricted by social expectations or rigid "shoulds". This openness allowed me to question and seek my own path, but it also left me grappling with certain aspects of my identity, especially in the aftermath of childhood experiences that caused me to question, at the time, who I was.

From an early age I was bullied, and this caused me to suffer a profound loss of identity. By "loss of identity", I mean that it felt as though a part of my spirit – my very essence – had been diminished. It's dramatic, I know, but when your spirit feels wounded, your ability to express yourself authentically is stifled. In other words, when you are fully self-expressed, you are being your authentic self: this is where you feel abuzz, your heart sings, and everything you feel and want to express flows naturally. But in my case, childhood bullying limited my ability to self-express, and caused me to constrict vocally and shrink energetically so that I took up less space and would not be seen, for fear of repercussion.

I was silenced, made to feel that I couldn't be who I truly was, that my thoughts and feelings didn't matter, that I was not wanted. I was so constricted that I couldn't communicate what I was feeling or what I wanted to say. This loss of identity in childhood carried over into my adult life, manifesting in my struggle to speak my truth. Whether it's verbal communication, written expression, or even sharing who I am with others, I've often found myself holding back, retreating into silence rather than risk criticism or rejection. Writing this book has been one of the biggest challenges I've faced because it forces me to confront that fear of vulnerability. By sharing my thoughts and beliefs and my personal inner workings, I'm opening myself up to rejection, which is something that I've avoided most of my life. But through this book, I'm going to finally relieve the internal pressure I've felt for so long – the pressure to suppress my true self. This is my way of voicing who I choose to be in this moment for everyone to see, and, in so doing, creating who I choose to be.

The bullying I experienced in childhood had a significant impact on my life. It instilled in me a deep sense of social anxiety, a fear of speaking out or being seen. I sometimes catch myself thinking that maybe I deserved it, that perhaps I wasn't humble enough, or that I somehow invited that treatment. But the truth is, no one deserves to have their unique vibration diminished. Logically, I understand that I gave others the power to take this, as the power to do so rests with me to relinquish. Still, this realisation is something I only know now as an adult; I never understood this concept as a child.

The best way for me to describe the bullying was it caused me to dim my light, to retreat inward, and it has taken me nearly thirty years to find my voice again. In school, I learned to silence myself, to shrink back in social situations, especially when I felt dominated or criticised. This pattern continued into adulthood, affecting my relationships and social interactions. I would withhold my thoughts and feelings out of fear that I wouldn't be loved or accepted, or that I would face rejection if I spoke my truth. Even in relationships, I struggled to speak up, fearing that I might lose the relationship if I expressed what I was truly feeling.

The merging of sex and love

This loss of identity also affected how I engaged with the world socially. By the time I finished school, I didn't have a strong sense of who I was or where I fit in. During my teenage years, this led me to enter into a relationship with an older man when I was very young – too young to fully understand the implications. In hindsight, I see that he took advantage of my situation. I was just a child, and the age difference added a layer of complexity to the relationship that I wasn't equipped to navigate.

But at the time, this older man provided me with something I desperately needed – an outlet, a way to escape the loneliness and isolation I felt during those difficult years. There are parts of me that now recognise that relationship for what it was: a coping mechanism, or a way to feel validated when I couldn't find that validation within myself or from my peers. My lack of social identity made me more susceptible to seeking comfort in the wrong places, and I would have likely pursued that path, even if my parents hadn't allowed it. It gave me access to a social environment that I wouldn't have otherwise had.

One of the lasting impacts of that relationship, however, was the subconscious entangling of sex with love. Because I was so young and lacked emotional maturity, I began to equate sexual intimacy with validation and love. I didn't fully understand the implications of what was happening at the time, but that early experience created a pattern in my subconscious mind. For many years afterwards, I believed that having sex was a way to feel loved or to receive affection, especially when emotional intimacy was lacking.

This subconscious patterning shaped many of my adult relationships, where I sought validation through physical intimacy rather than emotional connection. It took years of self-reflection and inner work to begin untangling this false association. I started to recognise that my desire for sex was often a misplaced desire for emotional closeness or validation. Once I understood this, I could begin reprogramming my thoughts around love, intimacy, and connection.

The role of the subconscious in identity formation

As you can see, there have been a number of experiences I have had throughout my life that effectively "programmed" my subconscious mind and identity. What's fascinating about identity is how deeply it is tied to our subconscious. The beliefs and thought patterns we hold within our subconscious mind are the building blocks of our identity. If we continue to feed our subconscious mind with old, limiting beliefs, nothing new can show up in our lives. But when we consciously choose to reprogram our thought patterns by choosing new beliefs, new actions, and new ways of being, we open the door to a new reality.

In this sense, identity is less about "who we are" and more about "who we are choosing to become". The subconscious mind plays a powerful role in this process. Once we plant the seeds of our new identity within the subconscious, it begins to work on autopilot, driving us towards actions and decisions that align with that identity. Over time, as we collect evidence that supports this new identity, it becomes part of who we are.

One of the most important lessons I've learned is that standing in your chosen identity requires strength and persistence. There will always be external influences – people who doubt you or circumstances that challenge you – but when you are clear on who you are and what you stand for, nothing can shake that foundation. Your identity is not dependent on the opinions or perceptions of others; it reflects your own inner truth.

There's a vibrational quality to identity too. When you stand firm in the vibration of who you choose to be, everything around you begins to align with that. It may not happen immediately, but with time and continuous action, the world will reflect the identity you have claimed for yourself. This process requires faith – faith in yourself, faith in the actions you're taking, and faith that the universe will respond.

The most powerful realisation I've had is that identity is fluid, flexible, and entirely within our control. Whether you've experienced a loss of identity through bullying, career changes, marriage breakdowns, children leaving home, or other life challenges, you have the power to build and create yourself at any moment. Identity is not something that is handed to you by the world; it is something you create and reinforce through your thoughts, actions, and beliefs. We are creators of our reality. By stepping into an identity we consciously choose, and by taking consistent action to support that choice, we can shape our lives in ways that reflect our true selves. The journey of identity is ongoing, and with every action, we have the opportunity to redefine who we are and how we show up in the world.

3

Understanding the Programming of Your Environment

In the last chapter, we talked about the subconscious mind and programming, and how the two are closely and deeply intertwined. There are many different sources of information and influences that will shape what the programming of our subconscious minds ends up looking like, but there is one in particular that we will be focusing on for now: the programming of our environments.

So often, we operate on autopilot, not realising that many of our beliefs and behaviours are shaped by societal norms, family upbringing, and cultural conditioning. But when we become aware of these patterns, we gain the power to change them. We can step out of the programming that no longer serves us and consciously create new patterns that align with who we truly are.

For me, understanding programming has given me the freedom to question the automatic beliefs I've held for so long. It's helped me recognise that much of what I considered to be "truth" was simply inherited or absorbed from my environment.

From a blank canvas to entrenched programming

Before we are born, in the most simplest form, you might like to think of the subconscious mind as being a completely blank canvas. It starts from a place of nothing. Because we have not yet been exposed to any outside influences, experiences, or programming, the subconscious mind will not have been shaped or influenced by the information that it will absorb.

Nonetheless, the more that we engage and interact within the world, the more our subconscious mind will begin to absorb information from our environment – that is, our surroundings, the people we interact with, and the broader world around us. This will then shape the way in which our subconscious mind is programmed, and the beliefs, perceptions, and automatic responses that we end up having as a result.

How our environment impacts our programming

There are so many different ways in which our surroundings and relationships with others can shape our thoughts, behaviours, and overall wellbeing – all of which play a role in the broader environmental programming piece. Often, we receive environmental programming through observation or what we are told to do (or what we see others doing), rather than actually experiencing the event. Effectively, we are soaking up all the beliefs, behaviours, and attitudes of our family members and the environment around us (including our culture, peers, and media) and storing this in our subconscious mind. Sometimes, we will then continue to accept that these deep-rooted beliefs and attitudes are simply just "the way things are" or "my beliefs", without ever really stopping to question them or if they belong to you.

For one thing, the spaces that we live in, work in, and spend our free time in can all have a significant impact on how we understand and engage with the world. Furthermore, they can have a big impact on our overall health, wellbeing, and mood. For example, if we spend a lot of time in cluttered, poorly organised, or chaotic spaces, we may end up feeling anxious and stressed, whereas if we spend time in a tidier, more organised space, we may feel calmer and less "all over the place" as a result (that said, some people do feel calmer and less anxious in messier, less organised environments). The habits of your family during your childhood and early years of development can also play a role in shaping your future habits. For instance, if while growing up your family always ordered takeout, this is likely to be a habit that continues to be ingrained into you in your adult life, whereas if your family always made homemade meals and made different food choices, you may be more likely to do this too as an adult.

The relationships and interactions we have with others and the kinds of people we surround ourselves with can similarly play a crucial role in shaping the programming of our subconscious minds. For example, if we are able to enjoy positive, supportive relationships with others, this can foster feelings of belonging and self-worth, whereas if we experience impactful or negative relationships, this can lead to stress and anxiety. The relationships and interactions that you have with people in a certain space or context can also shape the expectations, perceptions, or beliefs that you have about what similar interactions will look like in the future.

For example, if you plucked up the courage to ask someone out once and were laughed at and ridiculed, this may make you more reluctant or afraid to do the same again in future for fear of being ridiculed for a second time. This is another example of how an interaction you have had with another person within a particular context can shape your beliefs and behaviours within similar contexts.

Other influences that our environment can have on our subconscious mind and programming can include things like cultural norms (as certain beliefs, practices, values, and traditions are likely to be programmed into you as "the accepted thing to do" or "the right thing to do" from a young age) and the media that you consume. This could be news and other mainstream media sources, or it could be things like social media content and entertainment like TV shows, movies, and music. When we consume positive and inspiring content, this can foster positivity and empowering beliefs, expectations, and perceptions. On the other hand, when we consume negative or fear-based media, this can foster feelings of anxiety, stress, and worry, which will then go on to shape our future thoughts, actions, and behaviours.

I want to preface something here: each experience you have had may be labelled as good or bad depending on your perception, but the way you respond to the event is not inherently good or bad – it simply *is*. What I mean by this is that the way your mind works and the way you process experiences is neither positive nor negative: it just functions as it does.

This does not mean that I condone harmful actions such as physical violence – those actions are not acceptable and can have severe consequences. What I am trying to convey is that the *thoughts* themselves, before they manifest into action, are not good or bad. They are simply thoughts. The mind produces thoughts continuously, and those thoughts, by their very nature, are neutral until we assign them meaning or value based on our perspective.

You have the ability to consciously recognise a thought pattern and decide whether you want to change it. Whether you choose to alter a thought pattern, or decide to keep it, is your conscious decision. Nonetheless, that choice doesn't make the thought itself inherently good or bad. Rather, it is simply a product of your subconscious mind, shaped by past experiences, conditioning, and perceptions.

The thoughts that arise are generally beyond our immediate control. They are simply a reflection of our conditioning and subconscious patterns. It is through awareness that we gain the power to decide how to respond and whether to reinforce those thought patterns or to change them. This is a conscious process that allows us to take ownership of our reality.

It is important to note that what I am describing differs from considerations involving mental health. Mental health conditions can significantly affect the way thoughts arise and how one responds to them, often requiring professional support. What I am addressing here is the general nature of thoughts as they arise in everyday life, recognising that they are neutral and that it is our perception and response that give them meaning.

In recognising that thoughts are neither good nor bad, we create space to observe them without judgement. This allows us to approach them with curiosity and compassion rather than resistance or attachment. It gives us the power to consciously decide whether those thoughts align with the life we wish to create, and if not, we can choose to gently shift them. The real power lies not in the thoughts themselves, but in the ability to consciously decide how we engage with them.

Imprinting

Again, so much of this environmental programming goes back to what we experience and are taught during our childhood. This is because, during this early stage of development, much of the programming that takes place will shape how we interact with and understand the world as we get older. In child development, you will often hear this early stage of development referred to as the "imprinting phase", which takes place within a child's first few years of life. This time of our lives is a critical period, because it is when we form many attachments to others and also absorb a lot of information from our environment and the world around us, which will shape our future thoughts, feelings, and behaviours.

For one thing, it is during this imprinting stage that children will develop a certain attachment style based on their interactions with their parents or caregivers. When a child's parents or caregivers are loving and responsive, the child experiences a secure attachment style, which sets them up for healthy emotional development and relationships with others. Conversely, if a child does not have access to a loving and responsive parent or caregiver, or their needs are neglected in some way, they are more likely to develop an insecure attachment style, which can impact their ability to form relationships later in life. This may mean that they are less willing to explore their environment and the world around them than children with a secure attachment style (who see their parent or caregiver as being a secure base, whilst still being confident to explore and experience the world). They may also struggle to express and manage their emotions in a positive way, experience challenges with their emotional and social development, as well as struggle with intimacy and trust in their adult relationships. All of these things are examples of how this critical imprinting stage can shape the information or programming that we have stored in our subconscious minds from a very early age.

Imprinting is such a fascinating and powerful concept. From a very early age, even before we are fully aware of ourselves, we begin absorbing and internalising the environment around us. This imprinting is part of the subconscious programming that shapes our beliefs, behaviours, and emotional responses as we grow older. It's the foundation upon which we build our identity, relationships, and worldview.

In my case, part of my imprinting came from my relationship with my mother, which was complicated and layered. As a child, I often felt disconnected from her. It wasn't that I felt unloved – I knew she loved me – but there was an underlying sense that I wasn't always wanted and I was hard work. This impression, though subtle, was profoundly impactful. My mother struggled with postnatal depression, which led to a lack of bonding between us – something I couldn't comprehend at the time, but have come to understand now.

My mother passed away in 2016, and though I deeply miss and love her, I've come to understand that much of what happened between us wasn't a reflection of me, but of her own internal struggle. She had tools and inherited patterns that shaped how she parented, and she did the best she could with what she had.

Becoming a mother myself brought these patterns into sharp focus. I realised I was terrified that I would replicate the same disconnection with my child – that I wouldn't be able to connect, and my child would feel the same sense of being unwanted or hard work. This fear was something I had to work through with the help of psychologists, because I understood how deeply that early imprinting had affected me.

Now, I can see that my mother's struggles were never about me. They reflected her own internal world, her exhaustion, and the challenges she faced as a parent. She was dealing with the weight of her own inherited beliefs, programming, and emotional experiences, and much of her difficulty in connecting with me was tied to those factors rather than anything I had done.

In hindsight, I can see how my early experiences with my mother shaped not only my relationship with her but also my ability to form secure attachments later in life. I developed an insecure attachment style, which made it difficult for me to express my emotions fully and connect with others in a meaningful way. This insecurity further impacted on my interactions with people, romantic partners, and even social groups. For years, I struggled to manage and express my emotions. Usually, I couldn't articulate what I was feeling on a deeper level, and I suspect that this inability to connect emotionally stemmed from those early childhood years. When we don't have secure attachment figures in our lives, we develop patterns of withdrawal or detachment as a form of protection. This manifested in a tendency for me to retreat when I felt emotionally vulnerable or when I didn't receive the response I desired from the other party.

The bullying I experienced during childhood only reinforced these patterns of withdrawal. I learned to remove myself from situations that felt unsafe, repeating the cycle of emotional disconnection that had begun at home. This repeated pattern of retreating in the face of emotional discomfort became a recurring theme in my life, affecting my ability to form meaningful relationships. And the truth is, I still get overwhelmed at times, especially in social situations.

As I've grown older, I've come to understand the power of this early imprinting and how it continues to shape my life. I've also come to terms with the fact that I am not bound by these early experiences. Though they formed the foundation of my subconscious beliefs, I now have the awareness and the tools to reprogram those beliefs and create new patterns if I choose.

What I've come to realise is that none of this is about blame. Parenting is incredibly challenging, and it's impossible to do it perfectly. My mother had her own struggles, and she navigated them with the tools she had and did the best she could. She couldn't have known how deeply those early years would shape me, just as none of us can fully comprehend the impact our actions have on our children until much later, and she would have never intentionally caused the impact if she were aware of what was going on.

In my own journey as a mother, I've worked hard to ensure that my child doesn't inherit the same patterns of disconnection that I experienced. I am more mindful of how I interact with my child, how I express love, and how I respond to emotional needs. At the same time though, I have a deep compassion for my mother and the struggles she faced. I've come to realise that she was a product of her own upbringing, her own imprinting, and her own limitations. Just as I am working to break the cycle for my child, my mother loved me in the best way she knew how, even if she might not have always been able to connect with me in the way I needed.

Imprinting, especially during childhood, is unavoidable. It happens to all of us. The experiences we have, the emotions we feel, and the relationships we build in our formative years all contribute to the subconscious patterns that guide us later in life. These patterns repeat, often unconsciously, until we bring awareness to them and consciously choose to change the cycle.

Understanding imprinting and how it shapes our lives has been a critical part of my healing journey. It has allowed me to recognise the patterns that no longer serve me and to consciously choose new ways of being. While I can't change the past, I can change how I respond to it, and I can choose to create a new reality for myself and my child.

I've also learned to forgive myself for the ways in which I've struggled in relationships, knowing that much of my behaviour was shaped by early experiences which were beyond my understanding to control at the time. With this awareness, I am gradually rewriting my story, moving from a place of insecurity and disconnection to one of love, connection, and secure attachment.

I've become more present too. Now, I know that there is an impact no matter what you do, no matter which way you choose to do something. I see it as a stone being thrown into a body of water. The impact of the interaction always makes a ripple; how long it permeates is influenced by the size of the stone you throw and the degree of the impact.

How colours, forms, and structures shape our programming and reality

I previously participated in a year-long course that radically changed my understanding of subconscious programming. This course opened my eyes to the ways we are influenced by seemingly simple things, like colours, forms, structures, and interactions within our environment. Through this, I came to understand how deeply our family, culture, and surroundings impact our subconscious thought patterns, shaping the way we interpret the world around us.

There are many things in our environment that we simply accept without question. They are given, not challenged. For example, one of the most common associations in Western culture is that boys are associated with the colour blue, while girls are associated with pink. These are ingrained in us from a young age, presented as fact, and rarely questioned. This course allowed me to dig deeper into these automatic associations and understand how they shape our subconscious.

One of the revelations during the course was the origin of the association between colours and gender. While most people now associate pink with girls and blue with boys, historically, it was the opposite. At one time, pink was considered a strong and masculine colour more suited for boys, while blue, seen as delicate and serene, was linked to girls. This colour-coding reversal happened over time, shaped by cultural changes and marketing influences.

This shift in understanding was eye-opening, because it made me realise how much of our "knowledge" is socially constructed. What we take as truth is often just an arbitrary decision that's been reinforced through repetition and cultural norms. We don't question it because it has been passed down to us as a societal rule, and we accept it without validation. This automatic acceptance of certain truths, without critically examining their origins, is at the core of subconscious programming.

What this course did was help me break down these subconscious patterns at a micro level, giving me the space to re-examine fixed views that I had held onto. This process freed up a lot of mental energy because it allowed me to see that many of my beliefs weren't based on truth, but on unexamined environmental programming. It wasn't just about colours or gender roles though – this applied to how I viewed the world in general. By dissecting these ingrained patterns, I was able to release rigid perspectives and invite a more fluid or feminine approach to life.

Our programming – whether it's about something as simple as colours or as complex as our beliefs about success, love, or happiness – shapes our reality. But when we consciously engage with these patterns, we gain the power to reshape them. When we allow ourselves to let go of rigid viewpoints, we invite a world of new possibilities into our reality.

Why your subconscious mind sticks to a pattern

So, why exactly is it that our subconscious minds become so set in their ways and determined to stick to these patterns in the first place? The answer is that the subconscious mind plays somewhat of a protective role for us, as it seeks safety and sticks to familiar patterns – for example, by making us want to keep inside our comfort zone because it feels safe and familiar, or reinforcing familiar patterns that produce a certain outcome – even when these are not beneficial for us.

You might like to think of it as being almost like a mental safety net, as it recognises patterns and potential threats based on our past interactions and experiences in the world, and triggers an automatic response to help keep us safe from danger. An example could be developing defence mechanisms like denial or the repression of emotions to help "keep us safe" from painful memories or emotions. Although this can sometimes be a positive thing, as it can help us to cope with challenging situations as well as maintain psychological stability, this can often end up doing us more harm than good in the long run and create *dis*-ease.

For example, when we become too comfortable with that sense of familiarity and are too hesitant to step outside our comfort zone, this can often impede our ability to grow and evolve as individuals. Usually, what happens is that instead of adapting to new situations and taking on new challenges, we find ourselves getting stuck in our ways and refusing to break out of those deeply ingrained patterns we have established over time – frequently because we are afraid of change or what will happen if we break out of those established beliefs or habits. All of this can keep us from reaching our full potential as individuals, and from enjoying the best possible sense of positive wellbeing.

Our environment is one of the biggest things that plays a role in creating these deep-seated beliefs and "set in stone" ways of thinking, acting, believing. Really, we can choose to think of our environment as a mirror, because the environments that we surround ourselves with and choose to engage in basically reflect, reinforce, and mirror back to us our inner programming. It is this that keeps us stuck in our ways and unable to grow and change – almost like a plant that has outgrown its too-small pot, leaving it stuck and unable to grow and flourish to reach its fullest potential.

Changing your programming

So, what exactly can we do when we find ourselves feeling stuck and limited by our beliefs? You can consciously change the programming. This means taking into account all of those beliefs, habits, and reflections that have been reinforced through your subconscious programming, and identifying those thoughts that you perceive are doing you more harm than good, or thoughts which are holding you back. We can then start to consciously reframe and change these patterns to create new ones that you consider to be more positive and empowering, and which bring you closer to achieving your conscious goals and highest possible sense of overall wellbeing.

Changing your perception is something we are also going to be looking at in more detail in the next chapter of this book. For now, the key thing to know is that the first step towards breaking the pattern is awareness. That means being able to look at your internal and external environment and the influences within that, and identify and recognise how these contribute to those limiting beliefs and patterns that you hold about yourself and the world around you. There are a range of different techniques that you can use to take this first step, including visualisation, positive affirmations, meditation, and other forms of therapy, such as emotion-focused therapy (EFT). Altering our environment and changing the kinds of people we surround ourselves by can likewise help us to become more aware of these limiting patterns, so we can then start changing them and reprogramming our subconscious.

The concept of self-talk is crucial here. We have two levels of internal dialogue – the conscious mind, where we actively think and process, and the subconscious mind, where patterns are stored and replayed without our awareness. These subconscious thought patterns shape our reality because what we focus on becomes reinforced. For example, when I held onto the belief that sex equals love, my subconscious mind would filter everything through that lens, and I would continue to create situations that confirmed that belief.

CHAPTER 3 - UNDERSTANDING THE PROGRAMMING OF YOUR ENVIRONMENT

During my thirties, I went to an intensive ten-day meditation camp, and had the experience of being shown all my relationship patterns and why I had chosen particular sexual partners and what the connection was between them. It appeared in my mind's eye as an old picture reel that would click over to the next relationship – click, click, click – until I had seen all my relationships, and those who had influenced who I had become and how they came to be present in my life at a particular time. What was present during this experience was my gratitude for these relationships, as each had influenced me and it gave me an understanding of why I was the way I was. Through this understanding, I became aware of why I had this pattern and why I kept repeating it.

When I began to consciously address these patterns, I started to rewire my subconscious mind. I made a conscious effort to separate sex from love and to build relationships based on emotional intimacy rather than physical validation. Once I began to take actions in alignment with my new beliefs, new patterns slowly emerged, and I started to create relationships where love was not contingent on physical intimacy, but expressed in deeper, more meaningful ways. This process wasn't easy, and it's still a work in progress. But with time, I've been able to cultivate healthier relationships where love isn't defined by physical intimacy. I've learned to recognise love in other forms, whether it's through emotional support, acts of kindness, or shared experiences.

It's also crucial that we start understanding the power of our thought patterns. The notion that what we focus on becomes our reality is central to the process of creation.

I've come to realise that even perceived negative thought patterns – those internal dialogues that tell us we aren't enough, that we don't deserve love, that we should stay silent – can manifest in our lives. When we focus on these thoughts, we take actions that align with them, reinforcing those patterns and creating more of the same. It's only by tuning into these thought patterns and consciously choosing to change them that we can create new realities for ourselves.

Whatever approach you decide to take, it's up to you. The key, though, is to find a way to help you shift from your perceived negative beliefs or habits to more empowering ones, and create new pathways in your subconscious that align better with your conscious goals. By becoming more aware of how your environment affects you and your subconscious programming, you can then move on to the next step, which is to become more resilient, develop new ways of thinking, and adopt healthier responses when engaging with different situations and triggers within your environment, but only when you choose.

Part 2

Changing Your Perception

4
Reinforcing Your Reality Through Perception

Once you recognise the limiting beliefs and environmental influences that you feel are limiting your self-expression, you can then start working on changing those patterns. One of the ways in which we can do this is by reinforcing our reality through perception, which challenges us to question our perspectives and reframe these in a new way.

Feedback loops

Before we can do this, though, it is important that we are first able to understand the different feedback loops that our subconscious minds have established over time as a means of protecting us. This is essential, as these feedback loops play a significant role in shaping our internal environment and sense of self-perception, and as an extension of this, our reinforcement of what we believe as a result of our current subconscious programming. There are several different types of feedback loops created by the subconscious:

- Behavioural feedback loops: A behavioural feedback loop is where you engage in a particular behaviour that kickstarts a cycle that leads to a particular outcome. This outcome can be perceived as either positive or negative. This outcome then reinforces the behaviour – either because it feels good or because it provides some kind of comfort, relief, or sense of perceived safety – which then encourages us to repeat the behaviour. An example could be procrastination (the behaviour), as putting off a stressful task may provide us with a sense of relief as we continue to avoid completing it. This usually means we end up repeating that behaviour, and just keep putting it off and putting it off.

- Emotional feedback loops: An emotional feedback loop is where a particular emotional response is triggered by either an external event or internal thought. Often, this kind of feedback loop can lead to avoidance, as if we avoid the perceived stressful event or thought that triggers that emotional response, it can help us to feel less anxious about it. Again, this then reinforces the connection between the two within our subconscious mind.
- Cognitive feedback loops: A cognitive feedback loop is where we have established thought or belief patterns (for example, "I'm not good enough" or "I don't deserve this"), which then trigger certain emotions or behaviours in response. These emotions and triggers then lead to experiences that confirm this thought or belief pattern we are experiencing – for example, if we avoid certain situations or don't pursue opportunities because we doubt ourselves or feel as though we are not good enough. This leads to an ongoing cycle of negative self-talk and other behaviours aligned with those beliefs, which again reinforces this belief within our subconscious.

- Environmental feedback loops: An environmental feedback loop is where something in our physical or social environment drives a particular thought or behaviour pattern within our subconscious programming. This could be peer pressure, the dynamics of your family, or simply the environment in which you live, work, or spend time. Within this environment, you are likely to receive either positive feedback (such as praise) or negative feedback (such as bullying or criticism), which will then continue to reinforce and encourage you to perform a particular behaviour. This is another example of how feedback loops can embed certain behaviours and beliefs within our subconscious mind.
- Self-perpetuating feedback loops: This is a type of feedback loop that is created through the experiences that we have in our early years of development, which we are then conditioned to believe. Often, this conditioning continues to impact us from our childhood all the way through our adult lives, as we continue to think or act in a certain way or hold certain beliefs based on the things we have been told. We will then continue to think or act in a way that reinforces these beliefs that we have. Again, this creates a recurring cycle that can be very difficult to break, as it is frequently so deeply entrenched in our sense of identity and perception of the world around us.

All of these feedback loops are cycles that will just continue repeating themselves again and again until we break them. Much of the time, this will result in the same situations appearing in your life over and over and over again, because each time you will continue to respond to the situation in exactly the same way as a result of this entrenched thought pattern or belief that has been instilled in you from a young age. The key thing to recognise here is that thought patterns in themselves are not bad – they are just patterns. Rather, the thing that we need to change is getting stuck in a way of thinking that is negative and destructive, and which is doing us more harm than good. Only then are we in a place where we can grow as individuals, and strive to reach our fullest potential without being hindered by those limiting beliefs that were previously holding us back.

Confirmation bias

The interesting thing about this is that, as humans, we tend to seek information that reinforces our pre-existing beliefs. This is what we call "confirmation bias", where the subconscious mind almost acts as a filter, as it is so stuck in its ways that it will often only let us "hear" information that aligns with our existing beliefs. This means that over time, we end up building up evidence in favour of the belief, which then reinforces and reaffirms it further, whilst ignoring any contradictory evidence that might disprove that belief.

For my part, confirmation bias manifested itself through the belief that no one liked me. In my case, this belief became a self-fulfilling prophecy. I would collect evidence, often subconsciously, to support that belief and reinforce it, while dismissing any indications that people did, in fact, like me. For example, my mother would sometimes say, "I love you, but sometimes I don't like you". This phrase, though seemingly innocent, stuck with me. It played out in my mind repeatedly and became the foundation for the belief that I wasn't liked; that there was something inherently wrong with me. This belief was further reinforced by the bullying I experienced, where I was regularly excluded or targeted, confirming to my subconscious that I wasn't liked.

As an adult, this belief continued to shape my social interactions. In group settings, especially those where I wasn't familiar with people, I would quickly fall into the thought pattern of "they don't like me" if I didn't receive what I considered adequate reinforcement – things like eye contact, friendly facial expressions, or engagement. When these social cues didn't align with my expectations, my subconscious would leap to the conclusion that I wasn't liked, which led me to withdraw further. I would stop putting myself out there, avoid deeper connection, and ultimately retreat into isolation.

This process of collecting evidence to support the belief that "no one likes me" became a pattern. At networking events, for example, I'd perceive someone's lack of immediate friendliness as a sign that they didn't like me. I'd retreat, not engage further, and the cycle would continue. I wouldn't open myself up to vulnerability, which I believe is necessary to truly connect with others. Instead, I'd close off and reinforce the belief that I wasn't liked, which eventually led to me distancing myself from the group entirely. Over time, I would stop attending those social situations altogether, cementing my isolation and reinforcing the belief.

What I've come to understand is that this pattern isn't unique to me. It's part of a larger human tendency to reinforce our existing beliefs through confirmation bias. The subconscious mind filters out anything that contradicts what it already believes, allowing us to build evidence that supports our view even if our perception of the worldview is negative or limiting.

This process of subconscious reinforcement starts early – often through imprinting in childhood – and unless we bring conscious awareness to it, it continues to shape our thoughts, behaviours, and interactions. In my case, it took years to recognise that the belief that "no one likes me" was not based on objective reality, but on a deeply ingrained subconscious pattern. When I finally began to challenge this belief, I was able to see the evidence to the contrary – that people *did* like me, and that my perception of social interactions was simply skewed by my own insecurities. In fact, people are so worried about themselves normally and how they are perceived that they often don't even notice the interaction at a deeper level.

Unravelling this belief has been one of the biggest pieces of personal work I've done. It required me to reprogram my subconscious mind, to actively look for evidence that supported a new belief: that I am liked and that people want to engage with me. This reprogramming wasn't easy, and it took time to override the old patterns. Interestingly though, what has become very apparent is that the "no one likes me" was actually more than that and what I was seeking is connection, something which was missing at a deeper level from my early childhood experiences with my mother.

What I've learned is that we have the power to change our subconscious patterns. By bringing awareness to them and challenging the beliefs that no longer serve us, we can begin to see the world in a new way. It's not that the world around us changes – it's that our perception of it shifts. And when our perception changes, the reality we experience changes as well.

The art of reframing

One of the most powerful ways I have discovered to unlock subconscious beliefs that hold us back is to step into vulnerability and ask for feedback from those around us. This is the art of reframing. This can be especially useful when trying to challenge and shift deep-seated beliefs such as "no one likes me" or "I'm not good enough". Often, these beliefs are formed in isolation, and without any external validation.

By opening yourself up to others' perspectives – whether through direct interviews or in more natural, vulnerable conversations – you gain insights that you might otherwise overlook. Asking others how they perceive you in specific situations can provide a much-needed reality check. What you perceive as rejection or indifference, for example, might be something entirely different, like the other person being distracted or preoccupied. When we open ourselves up to this kind of feedback, we allow new information to enter our subconscious that challenges the limiting beliefs we hold. Instead of assuming people don't like you, speaking vulnerably with them could reveal that, although they appreciate and enjoy your presence, they express this in a way that you do not naturally recognise.

The thing about this is that it is impossible for you to see this situation in another way and create a different outcome without first changing your point of view. For us to change our way of thinking and, by association, the emotional response and thought patterns that we have around a particular event or trigger, it is important that we are able to look at that event or trigger from different angles and see all of the possible points of view or "truths" that may or may not be true. We can then reframe our way of thinking and find a new, more positive angle that will help us to change our thinking and adopt healthier emotional responses and habits in the long run.

More ways to change your perception

Aside from reframing the way in which you think about a particular event or trigger, there are a number of other strategies that you can use to change your perception and foster more positive ways of thinking. Some of these strategies include:

- Using positive self-talk to shift the narrative: Self-talk can be a great way to alter your perception, because the way we talk to ourselves plays such a big role in shaping our beliefs and emotions. Modifying the narrative through self-talk can take some time and practice to master, but it is definitely possible. Rather than focusing on the negatives or what you can't do, try to consciously replace those thoughts with positive statements or affirmations that focus on your strengths. For example, instead of saying, "I can't do this", try telling yourself, "I am capable of overcoming challenges". By shifting your language in this way, you can alter your perception of yourself and your abilities, fostering a more empowering mindset.
- Practising mindfulness: Mindfulness is the practice of being fully present and aware within the present

moment, including where we are, what we're doing, and how we're feeling. By practising mindfulness, we can reflect on the kind of self-talk that we use to talk to ourselves, and mindfully decide to respond to different triggers or events in a different way. This practice is critical in transforming your way of thinking, as it strengthens your ability to reframe your thoughts and maintain a positive self-talk narrative. With enough practice, you will begin to notice that this new way of thinking starts to come more and more naturally to you, and that your programming will soon rewrite itself so that these new responses become automatic. With that being said, it is important to observe your automatic thoughts with kindness and without judgement, so that if you do ever fall back into your old patterns of negative thinking, you can gently and compassionately redirect your focus back to the positive.

- Choose your focus: This is something that is easier said than done, but with enough practice and determination, it is definitely possible to change your focus. Remember, what you focus on creates your perception and ultimately shapes your reality, so if you consistently dwell on certain experiences, you will continue to attract the same back into your life and your perception will be shaped by those thoughts. Instead, try consciously shifting your focus to foster a new or balanced way of thinking. Also, try and surround yourself with people who uplift you, engage in activities that bring you enjoyment, and experience environments that align with your desired mindset, as this can help you to foster and reinforce new beliefs that support your growth.

- Create new evidence: Earlier in this chapter, we touched on confirmation bias and how our subconscious tends to focus on building up evidence that supports our existing beliefs, even if those existing beliefs are limiting or not in our best interest. Instead, focus your energy on creating new evidence that better aligns with your conscious goals, perceptions, and reality, and reinforces the new beliefs or way of thinking you are wanting to foster. You might do this through meditation, daily gratitude activities, or journalling – all of which are great ways to change your focus points, celebrate the small wins, and create new subconscious patterning and perceptions. These activities also challenge you to identify the positive experiences and strengths in your life, which can help change your focus from what's lacking in your life to what you are good at or grateful for.
- Change your inner world: Our external reality tends to reflect the beliefs and perceptions that we hold internally. Sometimes, this can mean that when you get trapped in a limiting way of thinking and feeling, you attract the same back in the external world too. By changing your inner world, you will often notice that the same starts to show up externally, and you will start to see different outcomes happening in your external environment.
- Practise gratitude: It can sometimes be easy to get caught up in focusing on what we don't have or what we are lacking. Practising gratitude can be a great way to recognise what you already have and what you are grateful for, so that you are coming from a place of gratitude, rather than a place of scarcity. This can likewise be a powerful way to redirect your focus and discover new aspects of your life to appreciate, so that

you can look beyond the negative and see the positive. Not only can this help you to see your life through a more optimistic lens by refocusing on certain aspects in your life you want to recreate or have turn up again, it can also help to create new subconscious patterns that foster a more positive perception.

Finally, the biggest piece of advice that I can give you is to not get too caught up in the chaos. Life can be a pretty crazy and unpredictable thing, and we can often find ourselves ending up in complex, chaotic, high-pressure situations. Although a normal part of life, when the environment around us is chaotic, it can sometimes cause us to fall into our old patterns of thinking and we react to the breakdowns, which can then increase and add to our stress and confusion. This can then have a knock-on impact and thus a detrimental effect on our overall sense of wellbeing or cause *dis*-ease. For this reason, it is important that we know how to respond (not react) to this chaos and mayhem that comes with our day-to-day lives in a positive and productive way. This is something that we will be looking at in more detail later in this book.

5
The Perception of Mayhem – Redefining Chaos

As we touched on in the last chapter, the way in which we perceive and respond to the chaos and mayhem that we experience regularly in our day-to-day lives can play a major role in shaping our sense of perception, self-identity, and overall being. Life can often be unpredictable and complex, and at any given time, we can be facing all kinds of different events and stimuli all at once which can create a sense of overwhelm and disorder.

When we talk about perception, we are talking about how we make sense of and respond to these chaotic experiences. Quite often, when the environment around us is chaotic, we will find that our usual patterns of thinking and reacting to the breakdown can leave us feeling stressed, anxious, and confused. When we are in this stressed and confused mindset, we might find ourselves falling back into negative ways of thinking and old thought patterns, where we cannot help but focus on the negative aspects of the situation.

On the other hand, if we get into the practice of being mindful, present, and fully engaged within the moment, it will become easier for us to observe our thoughts and feelings without judgement, so that we can respond to and process chaotic situations in a healthier, more positive way. Practising mindfulness makes us more aware of the chaos, while at the same time shifts our perception to see things more clearly, recognise patterns, and respond in a more thoughtful, logical way rather than in an impulsive and reactive way. This can keep us from becoming stressed and overwhelmed, and make it easier for us to perceive our circumstances in a more balanced way.

My understanding of chaos and mayhem

I have been grappling with my perception of mayhem and feelings around chaos. In itself, chaos is purely a perception or context in which one lives. My intention is to redefine my relationship with the way I view chaos by altering my underlying perception and context to create a shift in context of what is occurring when chaos is perceived to exist in my reality.

My understanding of perception and context is purely intellectual. Really, this is not a "true" understanding, or in-body understanding or knowing. But still, the idea of chaos also has an energetic feeling of confusion, disorder or *disease* – that is, disruption to the systematic function and order of what I intellectualise and perceive as structure. This perceived confusion is something which we, as human beings, like to label in order to communicate the impact of something that we cannot comprehend through language. It is almost as if we are trying to find order in the chaos through labelling, to enable effective communication and keep the perceived chaos in existence for common purpose. When chaos doesn't fit our expected pattern of understanding or our intellectual structure of our existence in the world, it is almost as if we resist the chaos and force the flow into a means of existing instead of being.

It appears to me that our perception of chaos is something which is built up from prior knowledge, meaning perception comes from memory and past conversations and events that have occurred. Context, on the other hand, appears to come from environmental stimuli. We can also consider context as being an individualised field in which everything exists. This individual field then influences or affects the meaning or effect of the event occurring.

What's interesting is that, in Latin, the definition of context comes from *contextus* – a masculine gender noun for how something is made, and how structure and fabric are woven together as parts to create a whole. This, in itself, suggests that perhaps it is masculine or the dominant context that allows things or vibrational patterns to exist. On the other hand, in Latin, perception comes from a feminine gender noun that means to receive, collect, and gather understanding through logic and understanding, with this being the intellectual mind. So, how do perception, context, and comprehension define each other? Do they all exist separately, or do they need each other to exist?

Personally, I think that my desire to communicate this underlying feeling as chaos is actually derived from my perception, as my language has past-based apprehension, highlighted by my need to label the feeling as chaos. For me, there's a feeling of anxiety attached to this definition. I'm chuckling now, because I'm still describing it as chaos, but it can actually only occur as chaos, so maybe the language which is used to communicate this needs to be redefined. Maybe chaos should be communicated as structure, and understanding as organised frequency and vibration. Maybe, in effect, what I am trying to do is to tame and control the chaos by defining it as chaos.

Ask yourself, what is chaos to you? If you label it through language, also allow yourself to experience it as a body sensation. Perhaps you can ask others what their perception of chaos might be to explore the idea of chaos and how it occurs more deeply. Chaos, in itself, means different things to different people. An event that one person sees as chaos may be viewed differently by someone else who may not even see it as being chaos, so language only really works to communicate chaos when we are communicating with another person who shares our same context. So, if chaos means different things to different people, this must then mean they have a different perception or context. So, when we use the word chaos in language, it is really just to communicate an underlying feeling which is occurring, since chaos is an individual, and thus subjective, understanding. Could the chaos be as simple as a feeling of anxiety, worry, or another emotion?

In addition, when we talk about chaos as being the rationale of worries, this is a past-based conversation, but when we talk about it as anxiety, this is future based, which leads to the question: does chaos occur in the past or in the present? In the immediate moment of the present, being the now, does chaos exist? For my part, I know that I can experience chaos from emotional feelings which are perceived to exist in that moment. Something does occur in the moment, however, I'm questioning whether that feeling of chaos which is happening is due to my lack of control, which is a past-based conversation. Is the chaos occurring because I have anxiety about what is occurring and what could happen in the future, given my past-based understanding of what occurred? So, if chaos itself is not present in the present, does chaos really exist?

Transforming how I see and experience chaos

A couple of years ago, I was fortunate enough to be involved in an intensive year-long program that was designed to help us, as humans, become more comfortable with the presence of perceived chaos. What was amazing to see was how much my perception shifted and transformed, compared to when I first started the program and when I completed it. On the first day of the program, the overwhelming nature of what I was thrown into caused a good deal of internal chatter due to the perceived lack of direction and mayhem. It caused my identity to go ballistic and it was screaming because it wanted control. I felt so overwhelmed that I broke down and cried, stamping my feet like a child and communicating my upset with anyone that would listen. By the time I completed the course a year later, I had a far different mindset. By that time, there were new participants entering the same program and environment who were going through a similar experience to what I had had twelve months prior. This allowed me to have empathy for those people who were just entering the program as I was now in a space where the chaos had become easier to navigate and an intellectual shift in my context had occurred. My energetic field and context for experiencing the chaos had changed.

What is becoming clear to me is that my view of chaos is defined by the language that I use, which suggests that it is something that is out of my control and something which has a negative connotation in my worldview. My need to explore and grapple with the chaos is a means for me to control, understand, and put the chaos into a fixed picture view. I can clearly see I am not okay with chaos, purely based on the language that I use to describe and talk about it. So, could the feeling of energetic freedom be as simple as accepting how I engage and relate to the chaos?

I am now at a place where I am so grateful for my perception of mayhem and the intellectual unstructured chaos I perceive in the environment around me. Before, I never understood that chaos is what allows me to grow through the experience of the world around me, and without life's mayhem, I wouldn't be who I am being today. Without my perceived view of chaos, I also won't be who I am tomorrow.

6
Being "in Communication"

In the last chapter, I talked about my understanding of chaos and mayhem, and how my perception of this has transformed quite significantly over the past couple of years. Something that I also touched on in the last chapter, which I want to talk about in a bit more detail now, is communication. Communication is very important, because I have become aware that if I am expressing a communication to someone, the intention of the underlying communication could simply just be communication. For example, if I were to communicate my understanding of chaos to someone who speaks a different language or who was from another planet, they may not comprehend the words of language being spoken to them. Yet, my anxiety around the topic can still be communicated to them through the underlying emotional, energetic communication that can be perceived through my eyes, my tone, and my being.

What is communication?

Communication is such a varied, deep, and fascinating concept. It's a concept that I find overwhelming at times due to what it actually entails and represents, as well as the fact that it is something that can change so much and so rapidly in just one conversation. Communication is meant to be the imparting or exchange of information. We are taught from a young age that communication happens when you open your mouth and release a flood of words, which we expect the other person to listen to. Communication can certainly be verbal, but it can also be written, unspoken, energetic, cultural, or social.

The Latin word for communication is actually *communicare*, meaning to share through mutually understood signs, symbols, and semiotics – that is, how meaning is communicated. But the multifaceted and complex nature of communication is something that I think is often forgotten. Basic communication is something we are only taught to fit into societal norms and cultural upbringings (both learned and inherited), with the main emphasis being on common understanding.

Communication and miscommunication – and how it occurs for me

I love exploring how communication occurs for me. Already, I have dived into the idea of communication and what it is, what effective communication might look like, and how it unravels. I can also see how my perception of communication allows my identity to struggle to effectively communicate at various times, and that sometimes misunderstandings arise in my perspective because there is a quick emotional unravelling when I am not "being in communication".

That said, identifying this miscommunication still does not allow me to get out of my intellect and truly communicate; it sometimes plays out as a withdrawal, where I punish the other party by withholding all communication. This indicates that my subconscious still predominantly influences my interactions with others. I can now see that when I shut down in a social situation, it is not because I want to sever connections, but because I feel vulnerable and afraid of being misunderstood.

When I am in a monologue with myself, I allow the miscommunication to remain present. To be clear, the miscommunication does not have to be understood or even known. The recognition of a feeling of unease communicated via vulnerability highlights that a constriction of beingness has been experienced. When I am having a dialogue with another person who uses language through a common communication system, this misunderstanding can disappear. This allows the other person the opportunity to express what's really going on and give you context, understanding, and background, in turn, allowing the miscommunication to shift to communication based on understanding, compassion, empathy, love, and self-expression.

Finding a common communication system

In communication, one of the key challenges is finding a common communication system – a shared way of understanding and expressing thoughts, feelings, and ideas that both parties can relate to. This goes beyond just speaking the same language; it involves using words, symbols, or gestures that both people interpret in a similar way. It also includes having a mutual context or background that facilitates a deeper understanding – for example, understanding each other's cultural norms, personal experiences, or shared values can create a bridge for more meaningful dialogue. Emotional understanding is another crucial aspect of this system. When both parties are on the same page emotionally – actively listening, validating each other's feelings, and being open to vulnerability – they establish a foundation for true communication.

Without this shared system, miscommunication is likely to arise. Often, misunderstandings occur when cultural differences, personal biases, or emotional states create barriers, preventing a genuine exchange. In my experience, when I feel disconnected or misunderstood, it's usually because we haven't found a way to communicate that resonates with both of us. Finding a common communication system allows for a shift from intellectual disconnection to an empathetic, present conversation.

Misunderstandings and the missing context

I personally find that miscommunication happens on many levels and usually occurs when the other party lacks understanding of the context or when they feel they are not being heard. Both situations highlight that what is being miscommunicated is the underlying feeling or intent. This suggests that miscommunication occurs due to a lack of emotional awareness in the exchange, where the underlying feelings or intentions are not being fully heard or acknowledged.

Empathetic listening is, in my view, one of the biggest keys to preventing miscommunication and misunderstandings. Empathetic listening is about being fully present in the conversation, not just with words but with emotions, body language, and tone. It involves setting aside preconceived notions and actively seeking to understand the other person's perspective, even when it differs from our own. When we listen empathetically, we create a space for the speaker to express their true feelings and context. This practice allows for a deeper connection, transforming what might have been a misunderstanding into a moment of mutual understanding. Communication is, at its most profound level, not just about the exchange of words, but about connecting with the underlying emotions and intentions behind those words. By practising empathetic listening, we begin to bridge the gap between our and others' perceptions, moving from misunderstanding to genuine empathy.

The role of language in communication

Language in itself is an amazing way to try and communicate or share something with another person. Language is a spoken or written system of communication used by a particular group, such as a country or community, which may then be broken down further into subgroups and sub-subgroups, each of which may have their own language. Although we attempt to give and receive language constantly, this is not true communication. In effect, we have all types of communication present every day: verbal, unspoken, colours, symbols, active listening, and expressions.

Language plays a crucial role in our ability to move from misunderstanding to empathy. Regardless, while language is a powerful tool for expressing thoughts and emotions, it can also create barriers. Words carry different meanings, connotations, and cultural contexts, which can lead to confusion if they are not understood in the same way by both parties. For instance, when we use language that is rooted in our past experiences or cultural upbringing, we may unknowingly impose our own perceptions onto others. This can result in miscommunication, as the receiver might interpret the words differently through their unique lens.

However, when we become aware of these nuances, language becomes an avenue for connection rather than division. By consciously choosing words that express our true feelings and intentions, and by listening with the intent to understand rather than to respond, we open up the possibility for empathy. Language then shifts from being just a means of exchange to a bridge that allows us to step into another's experience, fostering a deeper, more meaningful communication.

Being "in communication"

Confusion occurring in communication is ever-present. We have terms in our language like "being in communication", "miscommunication", or "incommunicado". All the same, we are not taught what these descriptive words truly mean. For example, when has someone taught you how to "be in communication"? Before we look at what it means to be "in communication", though, let's start off by looking at what it means when you are "not in communication". When you are "not in communication" is when miscommunication and misunderstandings occur, which is what we were talking about before.

I've personally found that confusion in communication often surfaces in my relationship with my partner, Michael. My subconscious programming is to withdraw from communication, especially when I perceive it as confrontational. Michael, on the other hand, values open dialogue and prefers to address issues head-on. Whenever he raises a point, I instinctively feel as though my opinions and viewpoints are being attacked, and I find myself taking his words as criticism rather than an attempt to understand or connect. This dynamic has roots in my childhood, where I was frequently corrected for my thought patterns. I often had spiritual experiences that I struggled to communicate, and when I did try to express them, my father would either shut them down or respond so strongly that I felt my experience and perception were invalid. These early experiences taught me that speaking up was not safe, reinforcing my tendency to retreat in the face of perceived criticism. This gap between my inner experience and the words I use – or choose not to use – can lead to a breakdown in communication, highlighting how misunderstandings are not just about language, but about the unspoken emotional wounds that accompany it.

What I have found to be helpful has been to ask myself: what does communication feel like for me, versus just being "in language"? Can I differentiate between the two, and have I ever been in true communication with someone? This self-reflection has played a pivotal role in my personal growth. For a long time, I found myself stuck in a monologue, especially during disagreements. I would internalise my thoughts and retreat into silence. Whenever I felt hurt by something someone said, my initial reaction would be to retreat into my thoughts and replay the perceived criticism over and over. This internal monologue and narrator reinforced my belief that I was being attacked, which prevented me from engaging in open communication and heightened my negative feelings. Now, I have started making a conscious effort to actually open up the conversation with another person and move it from a monologue to a dialogue.

One instance that stands out was a particularly heated argument with Michael. I felt attacked and misunderstood, which triggered my instinct to shut down. This time, though, instead of retreating into my thoughts and letting the emotional turmoil take over, I decided to shift the interaction to a dialogue. I expressed my feelings of being criticised and acknowledged my tendency to withdraw when I felt threatened. To my surprise, this opened up a space for Michael to share his perspective without judgement. In that moment, I realised he was not attacking me, but simply trying to understand my viewpoint. By moving from a monologue of self-criticism to a dialogue of vulnerability, we were able to clear up the misunderstanding and foster a deeper sense of empathy between us. This experience taught me that true communication means stepping out of my internal narrative and being willing to engage openly with another person.

Another technique I've found to be effective is "reflective listening". When I sense that I am retreating inward and closing off, I consciously make an effort to verbalise my feelings to the other person. I might say, "I feel criticised when you say that, and it makes me want to shut down". This kind of statement opens up a dialogue, because it expresses my feelings without blaming the other person. In response, I also practise reflective listening by repeating what I hear from the other person to confirm my understanding. For instance, if Michael then says,

"I didn't mean to criticise you; I just wanted to share my perspective", I reflect back, "So, you were trying to share how you see things, not criticise me". This simple technique helps clarify intentions, making room for deeper understanding and empathy. It further shifts the focus from being defensive to being curious and present. By incorporating reflective listening into my interactions, I create an opportunity for both parties to feel heard and validated. In turn, this allows the conversation to transform from a battleground of misunderstandings into a space for mutual empathy and connection.

Finally, try sitting with and reflecting on what language actually is, and consider what in-body recognition feels like for you and how this is occurring in communication. I think that communication has an aliveness or a buzz, almost a euphoric sensation. It resonates through me; it is me. It is full self-expression, inquiry, and presence in listening. It can disappear as soon as it arrives when I step into my intellect, analyse, try to fix, and go into survival mode in the communication – in essence, stepping out of my beingness and into the realm of subconscious programming. This shift is significant, because it directly relates to the patterns ingrained in my subconscious. My subconscious programming, developed from past experiences and childhood conditioning, often tells me that it is not safe to be fully present in communication. It urges me to retreat into defensive monologues whenever I perceive a threat. For example, when I engage in conversation, my subconscious mind filters it through the lens of past situations where I felt my opinions were dismissed or criticised. This shapes my identity, leading me to believe that withdrawing and protecting myself is necessary to avoid being hurt.

Stepping out of "beingness" and into these subconscious patterns alters my perception of the present conversation. Rather than seeing it as an opportunity for genuine exchange, I perceive it as a potential conflict. Only by becoming aware of these automatic responses can I choose to stay in "beingness" and engage mindfully. It is through this conscious effort that I begin to rewrite old narratives, allowing my communication to be a true reflection of who I am now, rather than a reaction to who I was conditioned to be.

How would it look if we were all taught the essence of communication from birth?

Imagine a world where, instead of merely focusing on verbal skills and vocabulary, we were taught how to communicate with empathy and presence. In such a world, children would learn to identify their feelings, express them openly, and listen to others without judgement. They would be encouraged to understand the power of silence, body language, and tone of voice as part of the communication process.

In families, misunderstandings would be met with openness instead of anger or withdrawal. In workplaces, teams would thrive as individuals and feel safe expressing ideas and concerns, knowing they will be heard and valued. On a broader scale, communities and governments could engage in more effective dialogue, addressing complex issues with compassion and a willingness to understand diverse perspectives. Conflicts, whether personal or societal, would be approached not as battles to be won, but as opportunities for mutual growth and deeper connection.

In this imagined world, communication is far more than just the exchange of words; it becomes a dance of empathy, presence, and shared understanding. Teaching this from an early age would fundamentally change our perceptions and relationships, fostering a culture where misunderstanding gives way to connection and harmony. This looks like a whole new world of communicating to me, where we bring presence of beingness to speaking and listening.

7

Decluttering the Mind

When it comes to achieving that sense of beingness, there is another important piece of work to do, and that is to declutter the mind. Decluttering the mind means making space and completing your thought patterns so that other things can become the focus.

For most of my life, I could not understand the importance of this practice or what being consistent with it could do for my overall wellbeing and state of beingness. It was only when I started decluttering my mind as part of my spiritual practice that I started to become more aware and really getting rid of thoughts that were taking up my mental capacity and interfering with my creative process. Now, I can see that decluttering my mind has given me so much more calmness and creative space. Getting rid of the clutter has created space for me to become present, allowing me to step into the now and experience flow.

So, what, actually, is clutter?

By definition, the word "clutter" means to fill something with an untidy collection. The Latin word for clutter, *perstrepo*, means noise, bang about, drum, or rattle, which perfectly describes what mental clutter feels like when it's banging about in your brain.

For me, mental clutter means the noise or rattle of incomplete tasks and persistent thoughts that keep knocking on the door of my mind. These small, constant thoughts tug at my attention, making it difficult to focus and be present. I would often find myself agitated by these lingering thoughts – the dirty dishes, the need to pick up and put clothes away or the clutter around the house. They might seem insignificant, but they actively prevented me from finding momentum and settling into a state of presence and flow.

The more I thought about it, I also started to notice different levels of recurring thoughts:

- Simple action thoughts: These are the minor tasks, like putting the washing away or filling up the dog's water. They're simple and quick to resolve, and drop out of my mental space almost immediately once completed. Although minor, completing them creates a sense of freedom, as if that space is now open for something else.
- Medium-level thoughts: These thoughts have more texture and stickiness to them. They often revolve around emotional situations, like needing to speak to someone about an issue or processing a confusing reaction from a friend. These thoughts require a bit more action and can involve several steps to reach a resolution.
- Deep, sticky thoughts: These are the most dominant and overwhelming of all – the heavy, spiralling thoughts with an emotional pain body beneath them,

like "Why can't I secure a committed relationship?" or "Why can't I own a home to provide security?" These thoughts take up significant mental capacity and have a tendency to repeat themselves, like a movie playing on a loop.

I noticed that these deeper, recurring thoughts occupied around 40% of my mental capacity, whether they were at a loud or low volume. The thought patterns sit and spiral and they just continually knock, knock, knock at my mental headspace.

The impact of clutter on beingness

Throughout my journey to mental decluttering, I have asked myself why this clutter had the power to absorb space for creation. What I discovered is that clutter holds space; a decluttered environment allows what is unsaid to emerge, so for me, decluttering means everything has its place. However, I also realised that even when physical items are stashed away, they still hold space on an energetic level. It's like turning down the volume on a noisy radio – it's quieter but not silent. That's why it's not just about turning down the volume on intrusive thoughts, but about making them cease entirely.

The perception of clutter varies based on individual context. For example, someone with obsessive-compulsive tendencies may still perceive clutter even when it's out of sight, whereas others might have a lower "volume" for it. The noise volume in a space is influenced by one's mindset and perspective. It is this constant mental chatter that prevents the space of creation from coming forward.

In a conversation with my father about decluttering, he pointed out that academics generally have cluttered environments, while manual labourers tend to have immaculate homes. This made me consider whether manual labour allows for a clearer mental state through its simplicity and physical exhaustion. While this isn't universally true, it led me to realise that our personal space and environment often reflect our mental state and in fact might be connected.

The practice of decluttering

I occasionally refer to my mental clutter as "incompletions" or recurring thought patterns. It was only when I began to actively complete these thoughts as they arose that I truly understood the impact of decluttering. I became present to the importance of having a whole and organised space. Completing these small tasks allows me to sit down, be present, and actually write. My thoughts are no longer stuck in the future or reflecting on the past; instead, they exist in the present moment.

Through this process, I also recognised how my habits, such as drinking alcohol, would cloud my mental capacity and contribute to clutter. It was a form of self-sabotage, a way to avoid being present with my thoughts. I realised that this behaviour was comforting, yet maintained a low vibrational state, dragging me into past and future concerns rather than the now.

When I finally embraced the practice of mental decluttering, I experienced a state of mental peace that I never knew was possible. I came to understand that mental clutter is what pulls us away from the present, but by acknowledging and completing these recurring thoughts, we can create the space needed for presence and true beingness. Once the clutter had been cleared, I found I was no longer trapped in cycles of anxiety or past experiences. Now, I have the space to live and create fully in the present.

8

Removing Right and Wrong

As I continue my enquiry into belief, perception, and the creation of reality, I find myself questioning the concept of "right" and "wrong". These terms are so deeply ingrained in our thinking that they often feel absolute, as if there is an inherent truth to what is right and what is wrong. But what if these concepts are nothing more than perspectives? What if "right" and "wrong" are constructs we have built, influenced by our upbringing, culture, society, and experiences?

From an early age, we are taught to see the world through this lens of right and wrong. We are conditioned to believe that certain actions, behaviours, and choices are either good or bad, correct or incorrect. This duality provides structure and certainty in a world that often feels chaotic. But the more I reflect on this, the more I begin to see that right and wrong are not as clear-cut as I once thought. They are not universal truths, but rather products of our own perspectives and the context in which we view them.

In truth, the idea of right and wrong is incredibly subjective. What may seem right to one person can be entirely wrong to another, depending on their beliefs, values, and experiences. We are constantly making judgements based on our personal perspectives, usually unaware of how these judgements are shaped by the mental frameworks we have built over time.

I remember moments in my own life where I was certain I was in the right. I was standing on my pedestal of certainty, looking down on those who disagreed with me. But as I've reflected on those situations, I've realised that my sense of "rightness" came from my perspective at that time. It was shaped by my values, my upbringing, and my belief system. It wasn't an absolute truth; it was simply my truth. One situation that comes to mind is my time as a CFO. In that role, I often had to make decisions that I believed were "right" for the company. However, those decisions were not always perceived by others as right. Some viewed me as cold or unyielding. They couldn't see things from my perspective, and I couldn't see things from theirs. I was so wrapped up in my own sense of rightness that I didn't take the time to consider that there might be another way to view the situation.

The danger of absolute judgements

From childhood, we are taught to cling to these rigid notions of what's right and what's wrong. But doing so can limit our growth. When we attach ourselves to the idea that our way is the "correct" way, we close ourselves off to other perspectives. We create barriers that prevent us from understanding or empathising with others. This is something I struggled with for a long time – getting caught up in my own judgements, and believing that I had all the answers.

In truth, every judgement we make about what is right or wrong is filtered through the lens of our experiences, beliefs, and subconscious programming. It's like looking at the world through tinted glasses; we see things not as they are, but as we believe them to be. These beliefs are so deeply embedded in our subconscious that they become our reality, influencing how we perceive every situation.

But what happens when we start to let go of these rigid labels, and begin to see that right and wrong are not fixed, but fluid? The more I have explored this, the more I realise that these concepts change depending on the context. For example, a decision that seems wrong in one circumstance might be entirely right in another. It all depends on the perspective we bring to it.

I saw this fluidity first-hand during my time in India. While I was there, I observed various religious practices that didn't align with my personal beliefs. At first, I found myself judging these practices as "wrong" or "unnecessary". But as I spent more time immersed in the culture, I began to see things differently. I realised that what I had deemed "wrong" was actually a deeply meaningful part of their belief system. It wasn't about being right or wrong; it was about the context in which these practices existed.

This experience opened my eyes to the idea that right and wrong are not inherent qualities, but rather constructs shaped by our perspectives. We need to step back and examine our own judgements. When we do, we start to see that right and wrong are not universal; they are a choice we make in how we view a situation.

The beauty of recognising that right and wrong are not absolutes is that it gives us the power to choose our perspective. It allows us to shift the lens through which we view situations and people. We can choose to see things from a place of openness and curiosity rather than judgement. When we do this, we create space for growth, for understanding, and for new possibilities to emerge. This is not to say that we abandon our values or beliefs, and it's not to say that everything is permissible or that there are no standards. Rather, it is about understanding that our sense of right and wrong comes from our perspective. When we acknowledge this, we can begin to approach situations with more empathy and less rigidity, and allow ourselves to see the world through a new lens – one that is less judgemental and more open to the infinite possibilities that different perspectives can offer.

Personally, this realisation has been both liberating and challenging. It's liberating because it frees me from the need to be right all the time, and it allows me to explore other viewpoints and to see situations in a new light. At the same time, it's challenging because it requires me to confront my own biases and judgements. It also demands that I step outside my comfort zone and question the beliefs I have held for so long.

Moving beyond right and wrong

So, what does it mean to move beyond the concepts of right and wrong? It means choosing to view situations from a place of neutrality and curiosity. It means recognising that everyone has their own perspective, shaped by their unique experiences and beliefs and their own personal patterning. By letting go of the need to label things as right or wrong, we open ourselves up to a more nuanced understanding of the world.

In my own life, I have started to practise this by becoming more mindful of my judgements. When I find myself thinking that something is "wrong", I pause and ask myself, "Is it really wrong, or is it just different from what I believe?" This simple shift in perspective has allowed me to approach situations with more openness and engage in conversations that I might have previously dismissed.

At the end of the day, the concepts of right and wrong are choices. They are choices in how we view a situation, how we interpret actions, and how we relate to others. By recognising this, we reclaim our power. We can choose to hold onto rigid judgements, or we can choose to see things from a broader perspective. In my journey, I am learning to embrace this choice. I am learning that what I once saw as "wrong" may simply be a reflection of a different viewpoint, a different reality. And in recognising this, I am finding more peace and compassion in my interactions with others and within myself.

Part 3

Pulling Forward Your Reality

9

The Creation and Loss of Identity

One of the most profound things I've discovered over the years is that identity is not a fixed concept – it can be created and recreated at any moment. This revelation has been key to understanding how I navigated the significant moments of "loss of identity" in my life. A loss of identity happens when the current version of who you are, or who you believe yourself to be, no longer aligns with who you choose to be. It's when the identity you hold onto becomes unavailable or ineffective due to changes in your environment, roles, or patterns. It is your "I am" comments or how you describe yourself to others.

For me, the notion of identity is deeply intertwined with both my childhood and adult experiences. Growing up, I experienced bullying, which left me feeling like I had no identity. I was stripped of the ability to express who I truly was. Then, later in life, my identity as a CFO – a role I loved and found purpose in – was taken from me, leaving me once again feeling like I had no sense of self. Both of these experiences led me to a place where I had to redefine who I was. In essence, they were invitations to rebuild myself from the ground up and, in that process, I came to understand that identity is something we actively create in every moment.

Losing my identity

Throughout our lives, we will have spent a significant amount of time shaping and carving out an identity, and when this identity is changed or lost, we can sometimes experience an immense sense of grief and loss. I experienced this first-hand myself when I moved out of my role as CFO for a small ASX company. When this happened, I experienced a profound loss of identity. It felt as if I had been shattered into a million pieces. For three months, I sat on the couch crying, feeling utterly crushed. I couldn't breathe, let alone comprehend what life was supposed to be about. I had been defined by this role, and when it was gone, I was left questioning, "Who am I now?" My identity had been tied to being an executive, to the extent that I felt like I had lost the very essence of who I was. The job was more than a title to me; it was a reality I had created and invested in. When it was no longer mine, I felt like my sense of self had been taken away. I didn't know how to be anything else. Who was I if not that person? I fell into a trap of association, believing that my self-worth was tied to the role I played. Without it, I felt like nothing.

During this period of darkness, I struggled to make sense of my emotions. On some days, I would berate myself, thinking, "I shouldn't feel this way; others have it worse". But that internal dialogue only dismissed my own feelings. I became attached to the darkness and melancholy, and I coped by shutting down my emotions. I dealt with stress by becoming stony-faced, when I was crumbling inside. Was it depression, anxiety, or just a complete loss of identity? Perhaps it was all three but, later in my healing process, a bit of relief too, a sense that I could become whoever I wanted.

Looking back now, I can see that the attachment I had to my role as CFO wasn't just about the job itself; it was about how I saw myself in the world, communicated who I was and what I did. It became a way for me to establish an identity that I could hold onto, a way to counterbalance the effects of childhood bullying that had reduced my sense of self. Business gave me purpose and structure, a place where I could prove my worth. But when I was removed from the role – a familiar echo of my childhood bullying – I found myself spiralling. I had no anchor, no framework to identify with, and it left me questioning who I was.

The illusion of a fixed identity

Losing my identity was an extremely painful experience, but it also came with a powerful gift: the understanding that identity is not something static or predetermined. So often, we find ourselves falling into the trap of seeing our identity as something that is fixed or static. Actually though, it is something that we get to create, and something that we can change at our own will.

Identity can be redefined, and you can create a new identity as and when you choose. I have come to see that my reality and identity are not fixed. They are shaped by my thoughts, the roles I choose to step into, and the influences of those around me. This realisation is both liberating and a work in progress. I'm starting to recognise that our identity is fluid; we are not bound by the roles we take on. Instead, we have the power to create our own narrative. Our reality is shaped not just by how others see us, but by how we perceive ourselves and the narratives we construct within our minds. Understanding this has shown me that I can step out of old patterns and build a new identity aligned with my true self.

At its core, identity is about choice. We have the power within us to choose, daily, who we want to be. It's not just about how others see us, but about what we decide to embody and adopt as our truth. When we consciously choose an identity – whether it's one of empowerment, leadership, or compassion – we begin to take actions that align with that choice. Through these actions, we send out a message to the world, and eventually, the world reflects that message back to us.

In my case, I came to realise that I wasn't bound by external labels like "CFO" or the perceptions of others. I had the power to choose who I wanted to be and, through consistent action, could step into any identity I created for myself.

Redefining your identity

The process of identity creation is subtle but profound. It begins at a subconscious level, where we set our intentions and align our energy with the identity we want to adopt. This internal decision then gets reinforced through our actions. Every time we take a step that aligns with our chosen identity, we reinforce that narrative, building up evidence for ourselves and others. This is where the magic happens. Identity isn't something that is given to us by others; it's something we create and validate through our own consistent behaviour.

One of the trickiest aspects of identity creation is that the results, or the external validation of our new identity, may not appear immediately. This delay can often lead to doubt or frustration, as we might not see immediate reflection of our new self in the eyes of others or in the world around us. Nevertheless, what I've come to understand is that identity is solidified through continuous action. The evidence and validation we seek from the world will come, but you need commitment and persistence to be your new identity thorough continuous action.

It's easy to fall back into subconscious patterns, especially when others are slow to recognise the new identity you're creating. But the key is to remain present and to continuously embody the identity you have chosen, regardless of how others perceive you. Over time, through your unwavering actions, others will begin to see a change, some will reflect the identity that you are living out and some will no longer be present in your life.

Influences on our identity

The way in which we view the world helps to shape and create our reality. For some time, I have been reflecting on and questioning this notion, and the more I explore this, the more I begin to recognise the patterns emerging in my life. This became especially clear after watching *The Social Dilemma* on Netflix,[1] which talks about how social media algorithms reinforce specific belief patterns, creating a reality that's constantly fed back to us. It made me wonder:

---

[1] Orlowski, J. (Director). (2020). *The social dilemma* [Film]. Netflix.

are our own thought structures doing the same thing? Are they playing out our reality, continuously reinforcing the stories we tell ourselves? Could it be "garbage in, garbage out"? Could we, as human beings, be programs projecting our realities based on the narratives we carry? Could the stories that cycle through our minds be like a film reel, playing out on the projector of our lives? If that's the case, could we actually be the dictators of our narrative?

I think that the answer is yes to all of these questions, particularly when it comes to the identities and personas that we wear and present to the world. My dad often said, "We are but actors on stage, wearing a mask". For many years, I didn't fully understand what he meant, and sometimes I still grapple with this idea. Our identities and personas are all masks, and they can change daily, but sometimes they are created in response to how others perceive us. Essentially, we can declare who we want to be, and as long as our actions align with that declaration, others will accept it. But when our actions no longer match the persona, the mask starts to slip, revealing the truth of our being.

What I have come to realise is that, for years, I wore the mask of "ice maiden" – cold, focused, and strong – because I shut down my feelings to cope. It wasn't who I truly was, but it was the version of me that my environment called forth and it became part of the persona I adopted to survive. In hindsight, I realise that I was the one projecting this narrative, and in doing so, I created a reality that was not in alignment with my true self. So, could it be that the stories we tell ourselves and the narratives we inherit dictate how we respond to our circumstances?

The organisation I was a part of called forth a certain version of me, and that was the identity I stepped into. Nothing else could emerge apart from what that environment nurtured and expected. This realisation made me question the roles we take on and how they are influenced by external forces. Who we become is often shaped by those around us and the context within which we exist.

One thing I've been practising is expressing my feelings before they escalate to breaking point, by allowing myself to communicate openly rather than bottling up emotions until they burst out forcefully. In the past, I would suppress my frustration and anger, trying to be "nice" instead of expressing my true feelings. I earned the label of being cold or arrogant because I held back my emotions until they exploded out of me, landing like a tonne of bricks on those around me. I also grappled with my desire to be perceived as "nice". I had this fear of being seen as harsh, arrogant, or unkind, which led me to trying to be everyone's friend for fear people would not like me. But in hindsight, I realise that niceness was my downfall. There is a significant difference between niceness and kindness. Niceness is about reacting to others' expectations, while kindness is rooted in love and can still set boundaries. It's an ongoing practice, and I'm still learning to address my emotions with kindness instead of the reactive "niceness" on which I used to rely.

10

Being Your Word

There is another big realisation that I have had on my journey, and that is the importance of "being your word". Lately, I have become present to the fact that I have not been being my word. This wasn't just a fleeting thought or a casual observation – it was a deep knowing, an understanding of the impact that not being true to my word has had on my life.

I've been playing with the concept of "being your word", and how it's often tied to integrity and obligation, something people feel they *must* do. For many, it becomes about right and wrong, a set of rules to follow. But I'm discovering that being your word is something far greater – it isn't about morality or judgement. Being your word is a universal truth. It works in a way where you pull what you want forward in life via your word and your actions.

It doesn't carry with it the weight of right or wrong; rather, it is about alignment and strength of your commitment. It's about being in alignment with your truth and the requests you make to the universe. It's about making a request to the universe and aligning every part of your beingness with that request to allow it to manifest. When you're *being* your word, you're allowing what you desire to manifest through your actions, thoughts, and intentions. On the other hand, the absence of this alignment is what I've come to realise as "non-being" – an absence of something, or a disconnection from that vibrational truth. It means pulling forth a reality inconsistent with your desires and intentions.

In its simplest form, "being" means to exist, to embody a certain nature or essence. When we talk about a human "being", we're talking about the nature of who we are as individuals. "Beingness", in its purest sense, is the state of coming into existence. And what I've come to understand is that this coming into existence – this being – is a gradual process that continuously evolves and changes. It's the continuous unfolding of who we are and what we choose to bring into the world. And so, the act of "being your word" is the gradual pulling forth of reality, based on the commitments you hold and the actions you take to support them.

The power of programming and vibrational frequencies

In human existence, we operate on patterns – subconscious programming that is ingrained in us. These patterns are not random; they run on vibrational frequencies, cycling up and down, in and out. Our lives are like projections of these frequencies. They influence how we move through the world, how we interact with others, and how we manifest our desires.

When I'm not being my word, I am unconsciously pulling forward a reality that is inconsistent with my desires and requests to the universe. It could be as simple as this: when we make a request to the universe, we must align our beingness – our actions, thoughts, and vibrations – with that request. If there is a disconnect between what we say we want and how we behave, the universe responds accordingly.

An example from my own life is my commitment to being in a loving, committed relationship. I believe this is what I want, and I often express this desire both internally and externally. But when I examined my actions, I can see that they didn't align with this commitment. I noticed a pattern within myself where I was attracted to indifferent and unavailable men, and I'd become indifferent to behaviours that mattered to me. My pattern was to tolerate behaviours that went against my commitment to what I wanted. By staying in these relationships and not expressing my disappointment, I sent a message to the universe that this treatment was acceptable. My actions contradicted my request for a loving relationship, and my reality reflected that contradiction.

Effectively, my beingness was not in alignment with what I said I wanted. This misalignment was not just limited to my relationships; the same happened in various situations throughout my life. The reality I experienced was a reflection of where I was not being my word, where I was letting my boundaries blur, and where I allowed inconsistency between my actions and my desires.

This is very important, because in our human programming we operate on patterns that create our reality. These patterns, in essence, are vibrational frequencies that project back to us what we are embodying. When I am not being my word, I am not taking actions, and I am creating a reality that contradicts my true intentions. It's like sending out mixed signals to the universe.

The gap between intention and action

As I started to recognise this, it led me to deeper inquiries into the areas of my life where the results I desire – self-expression, relationships, spiritual growth – were not showing up. As I dug further into these areas, I realised that the problem wasn't external. It was within me. I wasn't being my word in the spaces that mattered most, particularly in my spiritual calling.

This is a prevalent theme in my life: not being my word. It's an insight that amazes me, how often I find myself out of alignment with what I say I want. The universe, it seems, responds not to our words, but to the vibration and energy we put out into the world, meaning the action or impact. Being your word isn't just about saying the right things – it's about being and living them. It's about allowing your actions to reflect the commitments you hold in your desires. If my actions and my beingness take on the embodiment of what I truly desire, then how can anything else show up?

The realisation hit me like a wave. I had been living a life where I wasn't truly being my word, and the results were clear. If the things I desire are not showing up in my life, where am I being inauthentic? Where am I not standing in my truth and letting my boundaries blur? Why is my beingness – the essence of who I am – not aligned with the commitments I claim to hold? In examining these questions, I saw clearly the rules I had set up for myself.

If I tell the world I want a committed relationship but the reality I experience is filled with uncommitted partners, the disconnect is not in the universe. It's in me. I'm not standing in my truth. I'm not being my word. And the universe reflects back the exact reality I have energetically communicated. If I tolerate indifference, then I am creating a space where commitment cannot exist.

Aligning your beingness with your desires

It became clear to me that something was not right – not because there was something *wrong*, but because I wasn't being clear with myself, the universe and/or god matter. When you're not being your word, the universe responds in kind. But when you step into alignment, and when your beingness reflects the truth of your desires, there is no room for anything else. It's the universal law of attraction in action. What you put out is what you receive.

As I continued this inquiry, I realised that my spiritual calling was another area where I wasn't fully embodying my truth. I wasn't being my word. This insight blew me away because it became so clear: I had been living a life where I wasn't being true to myself and the results spoke for themselves. If things aren't showing up in the way I want, the first question I must ask is, "Where am I out of alignment? Where am I not being my word?"

This revelation led me to start making conscious changes to my actions, my thoughts, and my beingness. It's a practice – a constant reminder to align my actions with the commitments I've made to myself and the universe. If I truly want something to show up in my life, I must *be* the embodiment of that desire. I must live it, breathe it, and allow no other energy to contradict it.

Being your word is not just about what you say though – it's about what you do and how you show up in the world. It's about embodying your commitments, aligning your actions with your desires, and standing firmly in your truth. When you are being your word, the universe has no choice but to respond to the vibration you are emitting.

The results you see in your life are a direct reflection of the energy you put out. If things aren't turning up as you desire, it's time to look within and ask yourself: "Where am I not being my word?" Because when you are in alignment – when your beingness reflects your truth – nothing else can show up but what you are truly seeking.

In this journey, I've learned that being your word is about more than just integrity – it's about creating a reality that aligns with your deepest desires. It's about standing in your power and knowing that the universe or god matter will meet you where you are.

Now, I am trying to focus more on "being my word" and ensuring that my beingness is in line with what I want reflected back to me. My spiritual journey has shown me that the results I seek will only manifest if I embody the universal truth of my desires. This means holding my boundaries, expressing my true feelings, and acting in alignment with the reality I wish to create. This has shifted my understanding of what it means to create my reality. Could it be that simply being my word – fully embodying what I say I want – pulls forth my commitment and reflects it back to me in existence? If my actions and beingness align with my intentions, how could anything else but that turn up in my life? Understanding this has shown me that I have the power to be whoever I choose, to step out of old narratives, and to build a new identity aligned with my true self.

11

Belief and The Purpose of Practice

In my journey of inquiry into perception and the creation of reality, I have come to realise that belief plays an immense role in shaping our subconscious patterns and bringing forth the reality that we wish to create. The idea that our belief system – those ingrained, subconscious thoughts – reinforces our view of reality has become increasingly clear to me. However, it was my experience in India that truly brought this concept into sharp focus.

When I was in India, I had the chance to observe religious groups engaged in continuous practices. From an outsider's perspective, some of these practices might seem unnecessary, or even a bit excessive – rituals, prayers, chants, and other daily routines performed with unwavering discipline and conviction. What became evident to me was that these acts, repeated day in and day out, served as a reinforcement mechanism for their unwavering belief. I saw people practising with such devotion that it seemed as though their belief had become second nature, ingrained into their very beings. They were not just performing rituals; they embodied the belief through their actions. For them, practice wasn't a chore or a means to an end; it was a way of life.

This realisation struck me deeply. Through this, I gained a massive insight into the importance of practice in building belief. It became clear that the power of practice lies not in the act itself, but in how it reinforces belief within the subconscious mind. I also came to understand that belief is not static; it is something we can actively shape and cultivate through conscious repetition. When we commit to a practice, we are essentially planting seeds in our subconscious – seeds that, over time, grow into a sturdy tree of belief. Without regular care and attention – without practice – those seeds cannot take root.

Belief is everything

Without belief, *nothing* else can manifest in our lives. Belief is what sets the subconscious tone for our actions, thoughts, and ultimately, our reality. It is the undercurrent of all that we do, often operating below the surface of our conscious awareness.

Those religious practices I observed in India were not just empty rituals, but powerful tools for embedding belief into the subconscious. Each practice, no matter how small, worked like a chisel, slowly and steadily carving belief into the minds of those who performed them. This is what got me thinking: what if the purpose of practice is not about the action itself, but about reinforcing the belief behind it?

I have come to view belief as a kind of subconscious programming. Just like a computer that runs on specific software, we operate on our beliefs which guide our perceptions, decisions, and actions. But here's the key insight: belief is not just something we can create out of thin air; it needs to be built and reinforced over time. This is where the power of practice comes in.

Belief and the subconscious mind

When I first considered the idea of practice, I thought of it as merely doing something repeatedly to get better at it. But my time in India shifted this perspective. I began to see practice as more than just a means to an end. It's about creating a consistent rhythm that embeds certain thoughts and ideas into the subconscious mind. It's like laying bricks to build a house; each practice is a brick that constructs the foundation of belief.

For example, in many religions, people engage in daily prayers, rituals, or meditation. To an outsider, these activities might seem repetitive, even pointless, especially if they don't align with our personal belief system. But the true purpose of these practices isn't necessarily about the specific words uttered or actions performed; it's about the subconscious reinforcement of a belief system. Each time a person kneels in prayer or participates in a ritual, they are reinforcing the belief that there is something greater than themselves. They are telling their subconscious mind, "This is real. This is true".

Our subconscious mind does not discern between what is real and what is imagined; it simply accepts what is consistently fed to it. This is why belief is so powerful. By engaging in practices, we feed the subconscious the same message repeatedly until it becomes embedded as truth. It's like a groove that deepens with every repetition, creating a path that the mind naturally follows.

CHAPTER 11 - BELIEF AND THE PURPOSE OF PRACTICE

In my own life, I have noticed that when I engage in practices consistently, my belief in what I am practising for becomes stronger. Whether it's setting intentions in the morning, visualising my goals, or even simple affirmations, the consistency of the practice builds my belief in the reality I am working to create. Without this reinforcement, it becomes all too easy for doubt, fear, and old subconscious patterns to take over.

Belief is the lens through which we see the world. If our beliefs are rooted in doubt, scarcity, or fear, then that is what we will encounter in our reality. All the same, when we build and reinforce beliefs that align with what we desire – abundance, love, peace – our subconscious begins to shape our reality to reflect those beliefs. This process doesn't happen overnight; it requires the consistent reinforcement that only practice can provide.

Think of it this way: if you were trying to strengthen a muscle, you wouldn't expect results after just one or two workouts. You would need to commit to regular exercise, gradually building strength over time. In the same way, belief must be built through regular practice. The more we engage in practices that reinforce our desired beliefs, the stronger they become.

In my own journey, I've come to realise that many of my old subconscious patterns were not serving me. They were rooted in beliefs that had been unconsciously adopted, often from past experiences or societal conditioning. To change these patterns, I needed to introduce new beliefs into my subconscious. But simply deciding to believe something different wasn't enough. I needed to practise. This meant adopting new daily routines: setting intentions, practising gratitude, and visualising my goals. These practices served as a way to consciously direct my thoughts and reinforce the beliefs I wanted to cultivate. At first, it felt awkward, almost forced. But over time, with consistency, I began to notice shifts in my thinking. My subconscious started to accept these new beliefs, and my reality began to reflect them.

The purpose of practice, then, is to build an unwavering belief. It is the continuous reinforcement of a message to the subconscious, saying, "This is what we believe; this is what we choose to create". Without this reinforcement, our subconscious is left to run on old, outdated patterns that may no longer serve us. Practice is the tool we use to reprogram our subconscious, to align it with the reality we want to manifest. What I observed in India is that those practices, regardless of their religious context, were powerful because they created an unshakeable belief. When belief becomes so ingrained that it no longer wavers, it sets the stage for that belief to shape reality. This is why belief is half the game. It is the foundation upon which everything else is built.

If we want to create change in our lives, it starts with building belief, and to build belief, we need to engage in practices that reinforce what we wish to manifest. This doesn't mean adopting religious rituals or beliefs that don't resonate with us. Rather, it's about finding practices that align with our intentions. It could be daily affirmations, meditation, visualisation, or even habits like journalling. What matters is the consistency and the *intention* behind the practice. By showing up every day and committing to these practices, we begin to feed new messages to our subconscious. Over time, these messages replace old patterns, creating a new foundation of belief that supports the reality we wish to experience. The practice itself becomes a form of devotion – not to an external idea, but to the belief we are building within ourselves.

12

The Journey of Surrender, Letting Go, and Embracing the Unknown

On your journey of pulling forward your reality, there will come a time when you have to surrender. In the journey of personal and spiritual evolution, few practices are as powerful as surrendering. Surrendering, in its truest form, is not an act of giving up; it is an intentional release – a conscious handover of control to something greater than ourselves, be it the universe, the network, or god matter. This act of letting go is a radical expression of trust that allows us to step back from rigid expectations and create space for life to unfold beyond the boundaries of our own subconscious patterning.

Surrender is a profound expression of freedom and personal power. When we let go of our need to control every detail, we step into a space of true possibility, free from the mental burdens that come with attachment. This doesn't mean passivity or avoidance; it's a commitment to open up to life's flow and potential. By choosing to hand over responsibility to a greater force, we free ourselves and become receptive to new insights, opportunities, and experiences that might otherwise remain hidden. Surrendering also removes the burden of control and hands over responsibility to another which eases the mind. It isn't about inaction; it's about redirecting our energy from control to trust. When we surrender, we move beyond ego-driven attachment and connect with a flow that is larger, deeper, and ultimately more connected and entwined than our immediate reality.

The art of surrender in life and business

In life and business, the art of surrender lies in balancing empowered action with trust. Imagine it as the interplay of masculine and feminine energies (which we will explore in more detail later), where the masculine is the structure and action we bring forward, and the feminine is the trust, the allowing, and the openness to what is possible beyond our current reality. When we act with intention whilst still releasing attachment to a specific outcome, we invite god matter, or universal energy, to align things in the way which is best for our forward journey. This balance between masculine and feminine energy was a hard lesson in my own journey. In my business, for example, I used to feel the need to control every aspect, pushing relentlessly towards my goals without ever pausing to let the process breathe. But I found that the more I held onto outcomes, the less space there was for natural growth, creativity, or unexpected support to come through. Surrendering allowed me to bring forward action with purpose, while trusting that the results would align in ways I couldn't always anticipate or control.

Surrender often means trusting that the steps you're taking will build momentum, even if the results aren't immediately visible. It's about choosing to focus on what's within your control – your actions and your intentions

– and releasing the need to control how you will achieve the final result. This surrender gives us resilience, helping us to stay committed to our vision without burning out or becoming disillusioned. When we stop clinging to every detail, we free ourselves to engage with life from a place of trust, inviting a higher knowing to intervene. This is when god matter meets god matter, allowing divine interaction to co-create our experiences in ways we couldn't achieve alone. Surrendering doesn't mean we stop caring about the outcome; it means we acknowledge that our efforts are only part of what is required to achieve the desired outcome. As we let go, we create space for divine timing, synchronicities, and a natural flow that allows things to unfold as they're meant to. In this space, we are no longer blocking the outcomes by rigidly holding onto our plans; we are creating the fluidity for outcomes to arrive in the best possible form, even if it's not the form we initially envisioned.

Surrendering means embracing the unknown, stepping into a space where the future is undefined and trusting that the journey will serve us. This is where we confront one of the deepest fears of the human mind – the fear of uncertainty. But when we let go of our obsession with predetermined outcomes, we make room for unexpected surprises.

This journey of surrender is one of connecting the dots backward. Looking back, we begin to see how moments of letting go opened doors we didn't even know existed. Our job, then, is not to dictate every detail, but to stay true to our vision or true desire (or underlying desire or "why"), take empowered steps, and then allow the universe or god matter to weave its own magic around our intentions.

During my time as a CFO, there was a period of intense pressure and emotional turbulence, to the point where I felt completely overwhelmed. In that space of exhaustion and vulnerability, I made the choice to surrender. I prayed, asking for guidance and for help in managing a situation that had grown beyond my ability to control. Shortly after, I was offered twelve months of unpaid leave. On the company's part, this may have been a strategic move, but ultimately it granted me the very freedom I was seeking. This was a pivotal moment in understanding the power of surrender. By releasing control, I made space for an unexpected outcome that granted me clarity, renewal, and an opportunity to reevaluate my path.

Surrender and being

This experience reinforced a powerful truth: surrender is not passive; it is one of the most active forms of trust. When we release our attachment to specific outcomes, we're not giving up on our desires. We're simply allowing the universe to align circumstances in ways that may be beyond our immediate understanding, but which are ultimately in our best interests.

A critical part of understanding surrender is knowing it does not absolve us of responsibility. We are active participants in creation, and surrender is simply a means of allowing and accepting god matter or universal energy to collaborate with us. Unfortunately, surrender can frequently be mistaken for passivity or avoidance. We've all heard phrases such as "If it's God's will, it will happen"; phrases which are commonly used to avoid action or taking responsibility for our choices. I believe true surrender is different. It's about identifying what we want, setting our intentions, taking aligned actions, and then releasing attachment to how things unfold. Surrender doesn't remove us from responsibility; it deepens our capacity for it. When we act with the knowledge that we are not solely responsible for every outcome, we liberate ourselves from fear and anxiety, making way for freedom and creativity to inspire our actions.

Throughout this book, we explore the importance of intention and the need for focus. Here, surrender complements these practices. We take actions towards our goals, but we don't force or detail every single step. We trust that our aligned intentions, once released into the universe or god matter, will bring back the right outcomes – often in ways that exceed our expectations or understanding, especially when we look backwards and reflect on all that has occurred.

Remember, surrender and letting go aren't destinations – they are continuous practices. They are the solutions to the subconscious mind's need for control, to the mind's tendency to cling to certainty. When we choose to surrender, we release the weight of our expectations, the fear of the unknown, and we accept that anything is possible beyond what we can see or logically understand. This brings us closer to our essence of being. Each moment of surrender is an affirmation of our faith in a reality greater than the visible, a commitment to trust in the unseen forces that guide our journey. This journey is not about being passive; it's about being receptive, allowing life to flow through us, and engaging with it fully, knowing that we are co-creators in something far bigger than us. When we see surrender as a path that

CHAPTER 12 - THE JOURNEY OF SURRENDER, LETTING GO, AND EMBRACING THE UNKNOWN

bridges our intentions with divine influence, we can recognise that we are most powerful when we act with purpose and release attachment to the outcome.

As you move forward, remember that surrender doesn't negate your dreams or ambitions; it amplifies them by allowing the universe or god matter to work alongside you. This is where true creation happens – where inspired action and divine timing merge, bringing into reality a life that is not only what you desire but, quite possibly, so much more than you could have imagined.

13

The Role of Gratitude

Gratitude is another thing that plays a key role in your ability to pull forth your reality. Gratitude, at its core, comes from the Latin word *gratus*, meaning "pleasing" or "thankful". It's from this root that we also derive words like "grace" and "gratuity", all of which carry a sense of receiving or giving thanks. *Gratus* is not merely about passively accepting something, but about recognising its value and reciprocating with appreciation. Gratitude is about creating a reciprocal relationship with life – acknowledging what we have and, in turn, allowing more to flow in. When we live in a state of *gratus*, we become open channels for abundance, love, and joy, as we continuously recognise and reinforce the positive aspects of our reality.

By understanding this deep-rooted meaning, we can begin to see how gratitude shapes our lives and connects directly to our subconscious mind. Gratitude isn't just about saying thank you; it's about consciously focusing on what we want to reinforce in our lives. It becomes a powerful tool for creating and shaping the very beliefs that influence our reality.

Gratitude and subconscious belief: the power of focus

For the longest time, I never really understood the purpose of gratitude work. To me, it felt like just another buzzword – something people throw around without truly grasping its depth. But as I've become more aware of how our subconscious beliefs shape our reality, I've started to realise that gratitude is about so much more than just saying thank you – it's a powerful tool for shifting focus and, by extension, reshaping our subconscious patterns.

Gratitude is not just about acknowledging the good things in life; it's about deliberately focusing on them so that they can reappear. The more we focus on what we're grateful for, the more we reinforce those things in our reality. In contrast, when we dwell on things we perceive as negative, we tend to reinforce and attract more of those negative experiences. This process is deeply tied to how our subconscious mind works.

The subconscious mind operates much like a magnet, pulling in experiences that align with the beliefs and the focus we hold. If you're constantly focusing on what's going wrong, your subconscious will align with that energy and create more of those experiences. But gratitude allows you to break that cycle. It redirects your focus to the positive aspects of your life, shifting the patterns that have been ingrained over time.

One of the key insights I've gained is that the events in our life – whether we label them as positive or negative – are inherently neutral. The value we assign to them is based on perception, and is often shaped by our past experiences or societal conditioning. This is where gratitude comes in as a form of reprogramming. When we practise gratitude, we're not just listing things we're thankful for; we're actively reprogramming our subconscious to focus on what we choose in our life, rather than what we don't.

The more we acknowledge and appreciate certain outcomes, events and emotions, the more evidence we gather that supports this viewpoint. It's a continuous loop of reinforcement, where our focus becomes sharper and our reality begins to shift to align with what we're grateful for. Gratitude serves as a conscious interruption to any thought patterns or limiting beliefs that keep us stuck in cycles of dissatisfaction.

It's important to remember that nothing in life is inherently negative or positive. That distinction exists only in our perception. When we step back and view events as they are, without attaching emotional labels to them, we free ourselves from the heavy burden of judgement. This change in perspective is crucial, because the moment we decide to change how we view something, the behaviour and thoughts around it begin to change as well.

Gratitude is, in many ways, an act of humility. It forces us to pause and acknowledge the things in our life that are working, even when other aspects feel like they're falling apart. It's not about ignoring the challenges, but about balancing them with an appreciation for what *is* going right.

My relationship with gratitude

For me, gratitude is a practice that I tend to turn to when I hit a low point. It's not always something I can sustain consistently, and that's something I struggle with. When

I'm feeling down or overwhelmed, practising gratitude helps me refocus and realign with the aspects of my life that are in flow. It's almost like hitting a reset button on my perspective.

I also notice that when things are going well, I often feel an overwhelming sense of gratitude for how my life is unfolding. In those moments, it's as though everything aligns, and I can see the evidence of my intentions manifesting before me. When everything is clicking into place is when gratitude feels the most natural, as it's impossible not to feel thankful for what's happening.

Even though my gratitude practice isn't as consistent as I'd like, I've realised that it's a tool I can turn to at any time to shift my perspective. Gratitude has become a way for me to stay present, to recognise the good that's already in my life, and to reinforce those positive experiences in my subconscious. It's like consciously tuning the magnet of my mind to attract more of what I desire, rather than what I fear.

14

Standing In Your Power: From Being Influenced to Influencing

Throughout this book, we've talked about some of the different ways in which our perceptions and realities may be shaped by external influences. For us to truly be able to pull forth our desired reality though, it is important that we are able to make the shift from being influenced to influencing, which means being more mindful of and taking a more active role in shaping our own perceptions and reality.

In my journey of self-discovery, I often found myself swayed by external influences. From childhood to adulthood, I navigated the world based on others' perceptions, societal norms, and the invisible guidelines that shaped my decisions. I played roles that aligned with what others expected of me, subconsciously allowing their influence to dictate my actions, choices, and even my identity. I allowed myself to be influenced by external factors without even realising it. I would adjust my actions to fit in, to be liked, or to avoid conflict. I compromised my own needs and desires because I feared rejection, judgement, or failure. This fear stemmed from my subconscious programming, the stories I had absorbed about what it means to be "good", "successful", or "worthy".

In my career, especially during my time as CFO, I found myself constantly adjusting to the expectations of others. Whether it was meeting the demands of the board, responding to the needs of the team, or fulfilling the image of a "successful executive", I was influenced by external forces dictating who I should be. I remember times when I felt an inner conflict, knowing that the decisions I was making weren't aligned with my true values. But I silenced that inner voice because I was more focused on meeting others' standards.

The problem with being influenced by others is that it strips away our authentic power. When we allow external influences to guide our actions, we disconnect from our true selves. We become actors in someone else's play, reading lines written by others, following a script we didn't choose. This creates a sense of internal dissonance, a feeling of being out of alignment. I often felt this in my life – a quiet nagging within, telling me that I was not being true to who I was.

It wasn't until I started to dig deeper into my patterns and beliefs that I started recognising this dynamic. I began to see how much of my life had been shaped by the influence of others. This realisation was both painful and liberating – painful because it meant acknowledging that I had given away my power, and liberating because it showed me that I had the power to take it back.

From then on, I started to explore what it meant to stand in my own power. This journey involved questioning the beliefs I had adopted from others, confronting the fears that kept me small, and stepping into a space where I could express my true self. It was not an easy process. There were moments of self-doubt, and moments where I wanted to retreat to the safety of being influenced because it felt familiar and comfortable. But each time I chose to stand firm, I felt a shift in my energy – a growing sense of empowerment.

Standing in your power: the move from reacting to creating

When you are influenced, you are in a reactive state, responding to the world around you based on external inputs. But when you stand in your power, you shift to a proactive state, where you consciously choose how to engage with the world. You become the one who sets the tone, the one who influences rather than being influenced.

To stand in your power means to take ownership of who you are, what you believe, and the reality you want to create. It's about changing from a passive state of reacting to the world around you, to an active state of creating and shaping your world. This transition requires a deep level of self-awareness and a commitment to consciously choose how you engage with the world. It's about recognising when you're being swayed by external forces and deciding to assert your influence instead.

This shift is not about controlling others or imposing your will. It's about being rooted in your own truth and letting that truth guide your actions. It's about being clear on your values, your desires, and your intentions, and allowing these to be the compass that steers your decisions. When you stand in your power, you become a creator of your reality. You step into the role of the scriptwriter, director, and actor, and start consciously shaping the narrative of your life.

CHAPTER 14 - STANDING IN YOUR POWER: FROM BEING INFLUENCED TO INFLUENCING

True influence is not about persuasion or manipulation; it's about embodiment. It's about embodying the values, beliefs, and energy that you wish to see in the world. When you stand in your power, you naturally influence others – not by telling them what to do, but by showing them through your own example. I have noticed that when I am in alignment with my own truth, people around me begin to respond differently. They sense the energy of conviction, confidence, and authenticity. It's not about projecting an image; it's about being so deeply connected to your own essence that others feel inspired by your presence. This is influence in its most authentic form. It is not forced; it is felt.

When you stand in your power and reclaim your role as the creator of your reality, you move from a state of being influenced by external forces to a state of influencing through your own presence, truth, and authenticity. Know who you are and what you stand for, and allow that truth to guide your actions. When you do this, you will no longer react to life; you will shape it. You will become a source of influence not by trying to change others, but by being so deeply rooted in your own truth that your very presence inspires change. This is the essence of true influence – the power that comes from within, from the conscious choice to live in alignment.

15
Trusting The Network and Meeting God Matter

As I've moved through my journey of beingness, I've come to recognise a deeper truth: we are all interconnected within an unseen network (universe) – a web of energy, intention, or consciousness. In this network, we are not merely isolated individuals; we are interconnected to each other, and impacted by each other. This connection is what I call god matter – an essence that is present in every one of us.

When I speak of god matter, I'm not referring to any specific religious belief or deity. Instead, I'm referring to the universal energy and divine spark that permeates everything. It is the force that animates us, flowing through every living being and particle. Trusting this network means trusting that this god matter within us and around us is constantly communicating, interacting, and responding. It's about realising that we are creators who set intentions, and that the universe meets those intentions in response.

God matter and the subconscious

This idea of god matter is closely tied to our subconscious patterning. I first came across the notion of the subconscious mind when connecting with the universal divine through the teachings of Neville Goddard.[2] He spoke of the subconscious as the medium through which our desires are expressed into reality. The subconscious does not distinguish between reality and imagination; it simply receives what we impress upon it and seeks to manifest that in the physical world. This god matter within us acts as a conduit, linking our inner thoughts and desires to the outer universe. When I think of this network or universe, it is an interconnected relationship between everything, how everything responds and reacts to each other, and how everything stays in motion due to the forces which push and pull each thing.

The subconscious mind, much like this god matter, is fluid, interconnected, and all-encompassing. It holds within it the power to shape reality, but it does so in connection with the universal network around us. When we set an intention or make a request to the universe, we are, in essence, communicating with this god matter within and around us. Our subconscious sets forth a vibration into the network, and the universe responds.

The ocean is a great analogy of this: a profound realisation about interconnectedness that I had once whilst I was on a plane, travelling across an ocean. As I gazed out at the vast expanse of water below, a thought came to me: the ocean is fluid, moving as one, yet composed of countless individual waves. Some waves clash and splash against one another in the middle of the ocean's depths, creating patterns of interaction. In that moment, I saw a parallel

---

[2] Goddard, N. (1952). *The power of awareness*. DeVorss & Company.

to our existence and the network of god matter. Just as the ocean is one body with individual waves that move, meet, and interact, so too does the divine network of god matter. When a request is made and communicated into this fluid matter, it sends out ripples that eventually meet with other waves of energy. Our desires, when impressed upon our subconscious, interact with the god matter in the universe, which responds by bringing forth the circumstances, people, and opportunities that align with our request.

Trusting the process

The subconscious is the divine medium that connects our inner world to the outer world. In this sense, we are creators, and our role as creators is to make the request – to impress our desires and intentions onto our subconscious mind. The act of creation begins within us, in our thoughts and beliefs, and these are then communicated into this network of god matter. Once we have made the request, it is up to the universe, or divine god matter, to fulfil that request. Our job is not to worry about how it will happen but to know that it will happen. Trust and knowing is crucial, because it allows the network to do its work. If we doubt or fear, we send conflicting vibrations into the network, disrupting the natural flow of god matter to meet our intention.

When I first began exploring the idea of god matter, I thought it was all about control – about consciously shaping my reality through sheer willpower. But over time, I've realised that it's more about making the request, setting the intention, taking inspired action and then trusting the network to respond. It's about recognising that we are connected to a vast, fluid mass of energy, and that this energy is always moving, interacting, and meeting our requests in ways we may not initially understand.

I have seen evidence of this interplay in my own life. There were moments when I set a clear intention, let go, and trusted the process, only to find that the right people, opportunities, and circumstances appeared, seemingly out of nowhere. It wasn't coincidence; it was the network responding. The god matter within me had connected with the god matter in others, aligning events to meet my request. Other times, I noticed that when I acted out of fear, doubt, or a need to control, things felt disjointed and resistant. My desires struggled to manifest because I was sending conflicting signals into the network. It was like stirring up turbulent waves in the ocean, disrupting the natural flow of god matter trying to meet my intention.

Trusting the network of god matter means letting go of the need to control every detail of how our desires will manifest. It requires us to understand that once we set an intention, we have already communicated it into the divine network. Our subconscious mind has received the message and sent it forth into the universe. From that point, our job is to remain open, receptive, and aligned with the belief that our request is being met. This process is akin to planting a seed. When we plant a seed in the soil, we do not need to dig it up every day to check if it's growing. We trust that the soil, water, and sunlight will nurture the seed and that, in time, it will sprout. Similarly, when we plant a desire – when we take an action or make a request to the network of god matter – we must trust that the universe will nurture and respond to it in its own time and way.

Trusting the network of god matter is ultimately an act of surrender. It is about acknowledging that we are part of a larger whole, a divine flow of energy that is constantly responding to our subconscious requests. Our role is to set our intentions, believe in the power of our requests, and release them into the network with trust. This trust is not passive; it requires active engagement with our subconscious mind, consciously setting intentions, and choosing to hold a belief that the outcome is here. It is the embodiment of faith to which the network of god matter will respond and meet our requests. And as we practise this trust, we begin to see that life is not just a series of random events but a divine interplay of connections meeting and responding to the god matter within us. When we truly trust the network, and trust that god matter is constantly meeting god matter, we open ourselves up to the full power of creation, allowing us to pull forth the reality that we desire.

16

Masculinity, Femininity, and How They Intertwine

The idea of masculine and feminine energy is one that we have talked about a lot throughout this book. The balance between masculine and feminine energy is an important one to understand, because the two are so deeply intertwined, and it is this combination of the two that will enable us to pull forth our desired reality.

In spirituality, masculine and feminine energy are qualities that exist within everyone, regardless of gender. These energies represent different aspects of existence, creativity, and consciousness.

Masculine energy (or masculinity) is associated with qualities like clarity, focus, and determination. It is focused on doing and achieving, and emphasises logic and reason, independence, leadership, achieving goals, being strong-willed, and having the drive to take action and initiative. Masculine energy is the type of energy that we use in spiritual practices when taking action, setting intentions, and putting in structure. Conversely, feminine energy (or femininity) is associated with qualities like empathy, connection, emotion, compassion, flow and healing. It is feminine energy that allows us to connect deeply with our emotions, open ourselves up to creativity and new ideas, nurture ourselves and our relationships with others, and embrace intuition and our inner wisdom. We use feminine energy during meditation, reflection, and introspection.

For us to achieve beingness and spiritual growth, it is essential that we strike a balance between the two. For us to experience a holistic and integrated approach to life and greater sense of wellbeing overall, it is not possible for us to be only one or the other. Rather, we must understand and embrace both masculine and feminine energies to enrich our spiritual journey and growth.

The balance of masculine and feminine energy

My experience in India is something that I have talked about a few times throughout this book. My time there had such a profound impact on me, not only because it taught me the importance of belief and practice but also because it offered me insight into the balance of masculine and feminine energy, and how they shape the way we experience life.

This wasn't so much about witnessing spiritual practices, but rather a deep realisation that struck when I entered any one of the many temples. The energy there helped me understand that masculine energy represents structure – rigid, fixed, and linear. It provides form and direction. But without the presence of feminine energy, which is fluid, adaptable, and intuitive, this structure becomes limiting. Nothing new can flow into it.

CHAPTER 16 - MASCULINITY, FEMININITY, AND HOW THEY INTERTWINE

I began to see that when masculine energy dominates, it creates boundaries and expectations for how things *must* show up. It dictates a fixed path, leaving little room for flexibility or spontaneity. This insight contrasted sharply with the concept of flow I was beginning to understand: feminine energy which, when allowed to intertwine with masculine structure, adds the element of fluidity. It's what allows life to unfold in unexpected ways, offering opportunities that rigid structures alone cannot create.

In India, I saw this in everything around me – the idea that while structure is necessary, it's the fluidity of feminine energy that brings things to life. Without that flow, everything becomes rigid. This realisation fundamentally shifted how I viewed the world. I understood that in order to fully experience life's potential, I needed to find balance between structure and fluidity. The masculine builds the foundation, but the feminine allows the flow of energy to fill that foundation, creating a fuller existence. This helped me see that to truly manifest and create in life, we must invite both energies to work together. It's not enough to simply build the structure and expect things to show up. We must additionally allow space for the feminine to bring movement and flow, enabling life to unfold in its own way, beyond the confines of our fixed ideas.

I came to understand how, when breaking down subconscious programming, fixed viewpoints are a form of masculine energy. Masculine energy, as I interpret it, is linear, structured, and rigid. When we hold a fixed viewpoint, we are essentially limiting how things can show up in our reality. We create boundaries around how we believe something should appear, and by doing so, we close ourselves off to the potential for anything outside that narrow expectation to manifest.

For example, if I have a fixed belief that success can only come through hard work and struggle, then I limit the ways in which success can show up in my life. I won't be open to opportunities that come easily or through unexpected avenues because my belief is fixed. This is the essence of masculine energy at play. It creates structure and boundaries, but it can also be limiting if left unexamined. On the other hand, when I change my perspective from fixed to fluid, I am tapping into feminine energy. Feminine energy is more intuitive, adaptable, and flowing. It doesn't need things to fit neatly into a box; it allows for multiple possibilities to exist at once. When I let go of the rigid beliefs I once held, I create space for new experiences, insights, and outcomes to emerge. This fluidity allows life to unfold in ways I may not have anticipated, offering me opportunities that would have otherwise been blocked by my fixed thinking.

By moving from fixed to fluid viewpoints, we allow new energy to enter our lives. This shift from masculine to feminine energy doesn't mean abandoning structure entirely – it just means creating flexibility within that structure. It's the idea that, while we need form and direction, we need openness and flow too. When we allow this balance, we open ourselves to a greater range of possibilities, and we invite experiences that are more aligned with our true desires and intentions.

This realisation was transformative for me. It allowed me to reframe how I viewed the world, how I interacted with people, and how I approached challenges. By acknowledging that I had been operating under certain subconscious patterns that were rigid and limiting, I was able to consciously choose a new way of being – one that embraced fluidity, adaptability, and openness to change. This has allowed me to embrace the unknown, to trust in the flow of life, and to release the need for control. By stepping into this space of openness and adaptability, I've learned that there is always more to discover, always more ways for things to show up.

Manifestation through feminine productivity

Manifesting our desires is often discussed in terms of linear productivity models, which tend to align more with masculine energy which is focused, structured, and goal-oriented. While these models have their place, I've learned that true manifestation, particularly for women, happens through feminine productivity. This involves being in flow, listening to intuition, and moving with the natural rhythms of life.

Feminine productivity does not dismiss structure; instead, it uses the masculine framework as a container for the fluidity of creative expression. Just as Indian temple carvings wove themselves around the solid stone, the feminine intertwines within the structure, bringing the vision to life in ways that cannot be planned or forced. This is the essence of manifestation through feminine energy: it is about aligning with your inner rhythms, trusting the process, and allowing your desires to flow naturally towards you within the space you have created.

In recent times, I've sensed the emergence of a collective feminine consciousness – a rising energy that is calling women to step into their power in a new way. This consciousness is not about rejecting the masculine, but about embracing the feminine aspects of collaboration, intuition, and holistic living. It's about creating a life where different roles – mother, businesswoman, creator, nurturer – are not compartmentalised but integrated. I've often grappled with the need to separate different parts of my life, feeling like I had to choose between being a businesswoman or a mother, a spiritual seeker or a practical planner. But the more I embrace this feminine consciousness, the more I see that my power lies in the integration of all these aspects. Holistic living means recognising that every part of my life is interconnected, and that the practices of centering, visioning, and setting intentions are not separate from my roles as a leader or a creator – rather, they are the very foundation upon which my life is built.

This shift towards collective feminine energy is about trusting and supporting other women, creating "safe villages", and fostering communal growth and exponential growth. It's about creating an energy that thrives in spaces where we can connect, share, and support each other, free from judgement or competition. In these spaces, old fears and wounds begin to heal.

How masculine and feminine energies are intertwined

During my travels to India, I had an epiphany that helped crystallise my understanding of the relationship between masculine and feminine energies. Standing in an ancient temple, I observed the intricate carvings on the walls – patterns so complex and beautiful that they seemed almost alive. These carvings appeared to dance upon the solid, unyielding stone structures of the temple. In that moment,

CHAPTER 16 - MASCULINITY, FEMININITY, AND HOW THEY INTERTWINE

I realised that the masculine energy is the structure – the unchanging, steady frame. The feminine, however, is the intricate pattern, rhythm, and beauty that intertwines within and around this structure.

This insight shifted my understanding of how these energies work within us. The masculine energy is what provides the framework, the boundaries, and the focus needed to give shape to our intentions and goals. It anchors our thoughts and ideas in time and space. On the other hand, the feminine energy is the flow, the creativity, and the intuition that brings life to those intentions. It's what makes the structure meaningful, vibrant, and beautiful.

In the context of our lives, masculine energy might represent the action plans, schedules, and strategies we create to move towards our goals. The feminine energy, meanwhile, is what fills those structures with purpose, intuition, and flexibility. It's what allows us to navigate our journey with grace and flow rather than rigid force. The problem arises when we become too anchored in the masculine, clinging to structure and control, or too lost in the feminine, floating aimlessly without a clear direction. True power and creation come from the harmonious dance between the two.

Achieving a balance between masculine and feminine energies is the key to manifesting a life that is aligned with our true selves. It is not about choosing one over the other, but about recognising how they intertwine to create a harmonious whole. The masculine gives us the structure to anchor our dreams in reality, while the feminine breathes life, colour, and movement into that structure. It is important that we embrace and tap into the power of both energies within us.

I like to think of it as a river bed, where the river itself is the masculine structure and the feminine is the way the water ebbs and flows. Both are god matter – they know where they are heading, and you need to trust it will deliver you to your outcome.

Anchoring ideas in time and space

This is something we've already touched on, but it's something I want to revisit again now as it's one of the biggest insights I've gained whilst working with both masculine and feminine energies. For us to be able to manifest our vision, both are needed. We set our intentions with the feminine, creating a vivid picture of our desires, and then anchor these intentions in the physical world using the masculine through action, timelines, and follow-through.

To me, this process is like making a promise to your future self. In my own practices, I use visualisation as a way of connecting with the future version of myself. I see myself clearly living in the reality I wish to create. When I anchor this vision in time and space by setting specific dates, outlining steps, and making commitments, I feel as if this future version of me reaches back, pulling me towards her. This interplay of energies creates a magnetic force that aligns my present actions with the reality I am creating.

Ultimately, the dance between masculine and feminine energies is about trust: trusting that the structure we create with the masculine is sufficient to hold our dreams; trusting that the flow of the feminine will bring beauty, intuition, and creativity into that structure; trusting the seasons and the transitions from winter to summer, from introspection to expression; and trusting the collective feminine consciousness that is rising within us and around us, urging us to live holistically and embrace the interconnectedness of all aspects of our lives. When we trust in both of these energies, we can co-create with the energies that form the wholeness of our being.

Transitioning through the seasons – the feminine journey

Our lives can be seen as a series of seasons, especially for women. We move through phases of vibrant growth and external expression which are like summer, into periods of quiet reflection and deep inner work, akin to winter. For a long time, I found myself resisting these natural cycles, trying to maintain a constant state of productivity and outward focus. But I have come to realise that each season has its purpose, and honouring these cycles is an expression of the feminine energy that lives within us. Winter represents those times of introspection, shadow work, or what some might call the "dark night of the soul". It's a period of pulling back, and allowing ourselves to go inward and face the aspects of our being that we often hide away. I used to see these moments as setbacks, as times when I wasn't "doing enough" or "achieving". That said, I've come to understand that these periods are not about stagnation; they are about renewal. They are a vital part of the process that allows the subsequent "summer" to be full of life, growth, and expression.

In my experience, this cyclical nature is deeply tied to the essence of feminine energy. Feminine energy is rhythmic and collaborative. It thrives in a collective, supportive environment, unlike the solo, linear approach generally associated with the masculine. This is not to say one is better than the other; both are necessary. But I believe that embracing these seasonal transitions and allowing the feminine energy to express itself fully in each phase is what creates true alignment with our inner selves and our vision for the future.

17
Breathwork, Trauma Lines, and Connectedness

For us to really experience our true sense of self, self-identity, and beingness, I think it is really important that we can come to terms and become comfortable with our physical, emotional, and social experiences. Really, we can think of this as achieving a true sense of connectedness. This means feeling a deep sense of belonging, empathy, and shared humanity with our selves, those around us, and the broader world and universe around us too.

One of my favourite techniques for achieving a greater sense of connectedness within oneself and with others is breathwork. Breathwork involves using various techniques that consciously control your breathing to improve mental, emotional, and physical wellbeing. Breathwork practices can involve simple breathing exercises and deep breathing, or they can be more structured and involve specific transformational practices. Breathwork isn't just a tool for relaxation though – it can be used as a gateway to a deeper understanding that allows us to transcend our physical reality and tap into a higher consciousness.

Engaging in breathwork can be a great way to enhance connectedness, as you will often discover a deeper sense of connection to both you and others around you. You will also become more aware of your own emotions, perceptions, and ways of knowing and understanding the world around you. Furthermore, breathwork can be a useful tool for processing emotions and overcoming trauma, as it allows you to access a deeper state of consciousness and facilitate the healing of trauma within yourself. Through breath, it is possible to release tensions and emotional blockages, and understand trauma lines – patterns of energy within the body that have been created by past traumatic experiences. Sometimes, trauma lines may manifest as physical tension, whereas other times they will manifest as emotional or psychological distress. Breathwork helps us to become more aware of where these blockages exist, so that we can then release the pent-up emotions and physical tension associated with these past traumas. Not only can it help us to become more "whole" within our sense of self, but this practice can also help us to reconnect with our bodies, become more aware of and process our traumas, and heal. All of this plays a role in creating that sense of connectedness within ourselves.

Meeting *Sonia*

I attended a breathwork workshop once, with the intention of being open to the experience. For me, the concept of frequency is much like tuning a television – adjusting it to access different channels. Many people associate frequency with the mind or even the third eye, a place of deeper awareness. Breathwork, as I experienced it, was about using breath to alter and raise the frequency of your body. We did this through a nasal breathing technique, a specific pattern of inhaling and exhaling through the nostrils. This practice resulted in a shift in my physical and energetic frequency, elevating me to a place I had never been before.

The experience unfolded as we completed our breathwork session, lying on our backs. As my frequency continued to rise, something extraordinary occurred. I encountered a being, an all-knowing female presence I've since called *Sonia*. Whether she was real in the physical sense, or a manifestation of my subconscious mind is unclear, but what I do know is that her presence was undeniable and profound.

She wasn't human in the traditional sense. Her form was more like a shimmering mirage, like water on a hot freeway, vibrating inside my direct field of vision. Yet, despite this ethereal appearance, there was no doubt she was a being of deep feminine energy. Her presence radiated love, wisdom, and an immense sense of knowing.

When *Sonia* appeared, it felt like we were instantly connected, as though I had known her for lifetimes. Her energy was undeniably feminine, not in a physical sense but in her vibration – her essence was soft yet powerful, wise yet nurturing. She didn't speak in the way we typically understand conversation; rather, the communication was an unspoken, instantaneous knowing.

Every question I had she answered and her answers were shared with me both in words and in an unspoken in-body knowing, which was a deeper, intuitive understanding being passed on.

What struck me the most was the immediate sense of connection. She wasn't inside me, but rather in front of me in my field of awareness. It was as if she hovered just outside my physical space, but our connection transcended the physical realm.

During our time together, *Sonia* shared insights that shook my understanding of reality. One of the most powerful lessons she conveyed was about the symbolism of the cross. She explained that the cross is more than a religious symbol – it represents the juncture between the physical and the spiritual, or the point at which they intersect. The cross is a symbol of the crossing over between these realms, a point where the physical world meets the unseen spiritual dimension. As she communicated this, I felt her physically move me, almost as though I were being guided through a series of positions or motions that mimicked the crossing itself. It was as though my body was being moved in alignment with the energy of the cross, blending the physical and spiritual in a way I had never experienced before.

Some might describe this as possession, and perhaps it was, but it didn't feel invasive or wrong. It wasn't an experience of control or manipulation, but rather an energetic merging – a guiding presence that allowed me to understand something profound about existence. In that moment, I realised how interconnected the physical and spiritual truly are.

Another key message she shared was around trauma, specifically how trauma is carried through familial lines. I came to understand that trauma isn't just emotional or mental – it's vibrational. It's something that's passed down, encoded into our very being through the subconscious and energetic patterns we inherit from our ancestors; it is already present in our makeup. This realisation opened my eyes to the deep layers of trauma that can exist within us, even when we're not consciously aware of it.

At one point, my mother and grandmother appeared, to the right behind *Sonia*. It was as if we were having a multi-generational conversation. My mother's presence was stronger, more engaged, while my grandmother's presence was quieter, adding her support without the need to communicate. Together, we spoke about trauma and the ways it has been passed down through our family. It became clear to me that the trauma lines I had inherited were a part of my legacy, but they didn't have to define my future. I was told that this cycle could end with me, that I had the power to break these patterns and move forward without carrying them into the future generation. It was a profound moment of understanding and release.

In this space, I was shown that time is not linear in the way we typically think of it. *Sonia* explained that time can be collapsed, that it can fold in on itself, and that we have the ability to move beyond our limited perceptions of it. This understanding shifted my perception of reality, showing me that the possibilities are far more fluid and open than I had ever imagined.

The entire experience was mind-blowing. It was so intense and so far beyond anything I had ever experienced that, honestly, I haven't returned to another breathwork workshop since. The encounter was extraordinary, but it also frightened me. The depth of the experience and the sheer magnitude of what was shared left me feeling overwhelmed. But I know that this fear is not a barrier; rather, it's a sign that there's more for me to explore when I am ready.

What this experience highlighted for me was how fluid the subconscious mind can be when we're open to it. My upbringing, particularly the openness to spiritual ideas that my father fostered, allowed me to be receptive to experiences like this. The fluidity of the subconscious, and the ability to tap into energies and beings beyond our physical world, is something that is available to all of us if we open ourselves to it.

Part 4

Creating Your Desired Reality

18

What You Really Want (And It's Not What You Think!) – Depths of Realisation

In our journey of self-discovery, we might find out that what we think we want isn't what we actually desire. We might believe we want a new car, a bigger house, a promotion, or even a particular relationship. But if we look closer, we realise these are merely symbols or stand-ins for the deeper desires that when tapped into will inspire us into action.

This chapter is an invitation to take a step back and explore what we really want on a conscious level. In the same way we've examined our subconscious programming and patterns, here, we will look at how our desires are shaped. Through the Levels of Why, we can begin to peel away the surface wants and reveal the true qualities and values that can be found underneath the desire.

We often hear stories of people rising from rags to riches only to find themselves back at square one, emotionally or spiritually, and then rediscovering what it truly means to be "rich". One thing I didn't really understand until recently was that true richness is no longer about material wealth but the quality of our lives, which has a texture or a feeling attached.

As we examine our own desires, we come to understand that achieving external milestones alone doesn't create fulfilment. For example, wanting a car or a promotion can be less about the object or title and more about what they represent – maybe freedom, confidence, or security. Understanding the underlying desire behind our goals is a powerful realisation that transforms the way we approach them.

The Levels of Why

To help uncover our true desires, I use an exercise I call the Levels of Why. This exercise invites us to ask, "Why do I want this?" repeatedly until we reveal the underlying values. Start with whatever comes up for you, even if it's only a surface-level goal. Continue to dig deeper each time you ask "Why?" By doing this, you're moving beyond your programmed desires and into your own authentic desires.

Let's take an example from my own journey with financial security. Initially, I believed that I wanted financial success to feel secure, but by applying the Levels of Why, I discovered I was truly seeking freedom – freedom of time and choice. In my case, true wealth was about the ability to spend time as I wished, with family, and not be forced into choices driven solely by financial constraints.

Here's how the breakdown of the desire might play out:

- Why do you want money? "Because I want financial security."

- Why do you want to feel secure? "Because I want to have freedom – the freedom to choose how I spend my time and make decisions without the constant pressure of financial constraints."

- Why do you want freedom? "Because freedom would allow me to focus on what truly matters to me, like spending time with my family, having meaningful experiences, and growing my business in a way that aligns with my values."

- Why do you want to focus on what truly matters to you? "Because when I focus on what truly matters, I feel a deeper sense of purpose. I want my life to feel purposeful, and I want my work to be something I'm passionate about, not something that I feel drains me."

- Why do you want to live a purposeful life and have meaningful work? "Because I want to experience fulfilment. I want to live in a way that brings me contentment, satisfaction, and a sense of connection with the people I care about."

- Why do you want to experience fulfilment and joy? "Because I want to feel alive and in flow. I want to feel that every moment I live and every choice I make is in alignment with what I am consciously creating, so that I am leading a life that's full of meaning, joy, and deep connection."

With each question, we dive deeper into our true desires, moving beyond the surface-level material goals to the underlying motivations that matter. Time and again, you will find that what you are really seeking isn't a physical thing but an experience, a feeling, or a state of being. Here are some examples of the true riches people often uncover through this exercise:

- Connection: a sense of belonging, love, and support from others.
- Freedom: the ability to choose how we spend our time and energy.
- Purpose in the now: the feeling that our actions have meaning and impact.
- Peace: a deep inner calm and mental clarity.
- Contentment: a sense of satisfaction and ease, and feeling fulfilled with what one has without wanting more.

These qualities are some of the true "riches" that lie beneath our desires. By understanding this, we allow ourselves to pursue goals that align with what we genuinely want to feel and experience, rather than endlessly chasing fleeting, external symbols.

My journey discovering freedom beyond financial goals

To help you better understand this idea of depths of realisation and uncovering your true desires, I wanted to share a personal example from when I started my own business. In starting my business, my goal was to achieve freedom, specifically the freedom of time. But at a certain point, I realised that my business wasn't providing this freedom; instead, it had created a schedule with even more obligations. The very freedom I sought seemed to slip further away. Through reflection, I recognised that I needed to shift my focus and intention – not just in my business, but also in the way I approached my life.

As discussed in the next chapter, where we will be looking at the power of intention and focus, what we focus on is what we bring into being. If I'm focused on tasks and stress, that's what I'm creating. But when I started changing my focus to true freedom and the actions to get there, I began to create more time for what I truly value. Understanding this core value of freedom and connection has allowed me to build a life that prioritises family, balance, and purpose.

Our desires are often shaped not by what we truly want but by societal, cultural, and generational programming. These subconscious patterns might not even belong to you, meaning that though you desire something, you may not understand why you desire it. Our environment tells us we should have certain things – a new car, a bigger house, the extra degree, or a specific lifestyle. We've been taught that these markers indicate success or are a must-have, but they can leave us unfulfilled when achieved.

I used to think that if I reached the "multi-hundred-thousand-dollar club", I would finally feel successful and complete. But when I reached that milestone, I found myself still searching, moving on to the next goal without feeling any real fulfilment. This reinforced to me that physical success indicators don't necessarily equate to happiness. True contentment comes from fulfilling your inner values. Don't get me wrong – nice things and access to cash is wonderful and can be stressful if not readily received when required. That said, what I am trying to portray is that material wealth is not the answer to all things in life.

CHAPTER 18 - WHAT YOU REALLY WANT (AND IT'S NOT WHAT YOU THINK!) – DEPTHS OF REALISATION

Understanding your true desires shifts how we set goals and prioritise our lives. By focusing on our core values, we can align our actions with the deeper qualities we wish to experience. This clarity of purpose allows us to create a life that feels rich in meaning and joy, rather than one dictated by superficial markers.

19

Power of Intention and Focus

In the last chapter, we talked about uncovering your true desires, and how we often think we want something material but in reality, these material items are just stand-ins for a much deeper, truer desire. In this chapter, we will explore how to direct our energy towards these meaningful goals. By applying focused intention, we can bring our true desires to life, creating a reality that resonates with our deepest values and aspirations.

The undeniable power of intention and focus is one of the most profound realisations I've had in both my personal and professional life. When we talk about subconscious patterning and recurring thought patterns, it's easy to get lost in and focused on the automatic continuous dialogue of what's constantly running through our minds. However, what truly manifests in our reality – what we bring into existence quickly and effectively – sometimes boils down to one simple thing: what we focus on and reinforce with masculine energy or structure becomes reality.

It may sound simplistic, but this concept of intention and focus holds immense power in shaping outcomes. Although a simple idea, what is difficult is bringing this behaviour into practice through daily focus on specific tasks which, when prioritised (based on your ultimate why – see prior activity), create a reality you want to live. Every day, we are bombarded with countless tasks, distractions, and opportunities. Our subconscious mind is constantly filtering through this information, prioritising based on what we consider to be important. There are many times when I procrastinate with certain activities over others that would create my desired outcome quicker, and I can get distracted easily with what I call "shiny objects", meaning I get distracted by the latest creative pursuit I am chasing and not completing other tasks to the end due to loss of interest, even though they would completely change my business and reality. Often, we do this unconsciously.

And here lies the key: what we give our energy and attention grows, and what we bring our focus to is what we create in our reality. This is the kicker, as what we focus on is what is created. Nothing else can turn up, apart from what you are focusing on; it is the only thing that can turn up in your perception of reality.

Focus and the role of subconscious programming

Subconscious programming is something we've talked about a lot throughout this book. Our subconscious mind is a powerful tool that processes information far more quickly than our conscious mind. It's constantly at work, identifying patterns, filtering experiences, and shaping our perceptions to create our reality. This is why subconscious programming is so significant to our daily reality. The thoughts and beliefs we focus on, whether positive or negative, get reinforced over time from different interactions and experiences being played out, often from the same viewpoint. Frequently, this means that nothing else can show up until you change the focus point.

Think about it: if your subconscious is programmed with a belief that "I'm not good enough", you will unconsciously seek out situations that reinforce that belief. Similarly, if your mind is focused on abundance or success, you'll find yourself more attuned to opportunities and actions that bring those beliefs into your reality. This is where intention comes in. By deliberately choosing what you focus on, you can shift the direction of your subconscious programming, and, in turn, your external reality.

Focusing on business and in life

This idea of subconscious programming is something that I see play out consistently in my business. When I have multiple projects or tasks on the go, it's easy to get scattered and make little progress on each of them. This is often because my focus is diluted. When you divide your attention across several tasks, each one only receives a fraction of your energy. This can lead to frustration, as nothing moves forward at the pace you want.

I've found that when I intentionally focus on just one task or goal, things change dramatically. It's as if the universe meets that intention with an equal force. By zoning in on one thing and giving it my full attention, I can bring it to completion much faster than if I were juggling five things at once. This doesn't mean multitasking is inherently bad, but it does mean that if you want to see results more quickly, focusing on one priority at a time is key.

In a way, focus is like a magnifying glass. It channels energy into one specific area, amplifying it. What you prioritise is what you create, so to me, this makes me question: if I am not prioritising, how will I achieve the outcome? This has meant reducing my work week from five days to four days. That said, even by taking all the steps necessary to achieve this outcome, everything will move at a much slower pace if I have not focused my energy on moving to a four-day week. But when my priority is focused, it is in my ability to create this shift.

The refining process

What's also fascinating about intention and focus is the refining process. The more you focus on something, the clearer and clearer it becomes. If you're working on a project or a personal goal, each time it comes up in your thoughts, you gain new insights, ways of approaching it, and new ways to refine your approach and move closer to the desired outcome. This refinement happens because your attention brings fresh ideas and perspectives. You start to see connections you hadn't noticed before, even in totally unrelated situations which you can apply to the situation you are trying to resolve, and solutions will start to emerge naturally. This allows your vision to become clear – so clear that you can see every piece of it.

This process is especially true in creative work or when you're solving complex problems. The more time and energy you give to a task, the more your subconscious mind works in the background to find innovative solutions or refine the details.

The dangers of divided focus

Conversely, when you spread your focus too thin, the opposite happens. Not only does everything slow down, but you also dilute the power of your intention. If you try to create five things at once or juggle too many priorities, you run the risk of achieving little in any area. This is because the energy you're putting out is fragmented. I often see this as trying to push five large boulders uphill at once. It might be near impossible to move five big boulders, but when you push one large boulder at a time to the top, five times, you will get the same result much more quickly – all boulders on top of the hill.

I've experienced this first-hand when I tried to complete multiple aspects of my business simultaneously, especially in the marketing side of the business. Nothing progressed as quickly as I wanted it to, and I felt stuck. But when I shifted my focus to just one priority and made sure that I finished that task before moving to the next, things started progressing much more smoothly and at a faster pace. It was as though the universe responded to my focus by aligning everything to support that one goal. To be clear here, I am not saying you should not have an action plan with the steps of what you want to achieve, with timing as to when you will focus on them. I am saying that working on all your marketing activity for the next year simultaneously will slow down the progress and you will likely not achieve any of the key tasks until the end of the year, instead of in each month/quarter. Similarly, you can have a few outcomes you wish to achieve; you just need to be conscious that they compete for your focus to become reality.

How to harness the power of intention and focus

To be able to properly harness the power of intention and focus, you first need clarity. What is it that you truly want? What is the one thing that, if accomplished, would have the greatest impact on your life or business? Once you have that clarity, set your intention or vision. Your intention is like a roadmap – it tells your subconscious mind and the universe where you want to go.

Then, commit to focusing on that one priority. This doesn't mean you ignore everything else, but it does mean you give your best energy to your top goal, or the one with the most impact that will support the outcome you want. By doing this, you accelerate the process of bringing it into reality. Each day, be present to the goal with focus and intention, refine it, and work on it.

The ripple effect

What's beautiful about intention and focus is the ripple effect that it has on the rest of your life. When you bring one project or goal to completion, it frees up your energy to move onto the next thing. This creates momentum. The more you focus and complete, the more empowered you feel, and the faster your future is created.

I see this in business when I complete a task and have learned things along the way that I then take with me to next project. This is the ripple, or the current actions that impact and influence your next action. It is part of the idea that you can't see the dots going forward; you can only connect them going backwards.

Focusing on what truly matters allows you to move through your life with purpose. Instead of being reactive and pulled in multiple directions, you become proactive, deciding where your energy flows and what you are going to focus on to achieve what you want. I think this is a critical consideration and one I did not understand for a long time. It is the idea of what you truly want and desire, and I think there is something missing in how a lot of people understand desire. What I mean by this is often you hear about people talking about wanting a car, house, boat, or money – but what people don't understand is the material things are providing something that is not what they "truly" want, and to identify that, you need to go deeper and ask yourself what I call the "levels of why" (discussed in prior chapter). There are material riches that we all want, but it is life's tapestry of richness which is different for each and every one of us. Only when we focus on what we truly want and take action that aligns with it, does life open up in new ways we have not previously experienced.

The power of intention and focus cannot be overstated, because what we focus on expands. The more intentional we are with our time and energy, the faster we can bring our ideas, goals, and desires into reality and create our desired richness.

Our subconscious mind will always work to create the outcomes we direct it towards, so the question is: what are you focusing on? Do you know what richness you desire? Are you scattering your energy across too many things, or are you directing it towards what matters most? The choice is yours.

20

Letting Go of Attachment

In the previous chapter, we talked about how intention and focus can bring us closer to achieving the reality that we desire. One realisation I've had on this journey of creation and being is that there is a critical difference between attachment and focus. While focus can accelerate the reality to create our goals, attachment can actually slow the process. It's a subtle yet powerful distinction that often gets overlooked, but understanding this difference has had a transformative impact on how I approach my goals and desires.

Attachment is when we cling to a specific outcome, sometimes with a sense of desperation or neediness. It's the feeling of needing something to happen in a certain way. When we become too attached, we create resistance rather than flow. We may believe that if things don't go exactly as planned, it's a failure or we're not on the right path. I like to think of this as fixed form – too much structure. What I mean by this is when we have attachment to a specific way something needs to turn up, we have a fixed and rigid viewpoint that is hard to change, which leaves little room for anything else to show up that could give us the same outcome. In earlier chapters, we discussed fixed views, meaning that when we process information using a certain view, it ends up only being this same fixed view that turns up in our reality. Attachment is almost like a fixed viewpoint where we see things from only one angle.

Attachment is deeply tied to our subconscious need for control. We attach ourselves to a particular vision or expectation and place all our happiness or self-worth on achieving that outcome, in the way it "should" turn up. The problem with attachment is that it creates tension both mentally and energetically. Instead of allowing things to unfold naturally, we try to force the outcome. And often, the more we cling, the more elusive the outcome becomes.

In business, attachment shows up when we fixate on a specific client deal, a project outcome, or even the validation we seek from others. We become so attached to the result that we lose sight in the immediate results and fail to see the bigger picture. It can cause stress and anxiety because we're emotionally tied to things happening exactly as we expect them to.

One of my looping patterns is survival and concern around cash and where it will come from. This pattern of attachment for the outcome only allows it to come up in the way I expect it to – not every other possible way it might, of which I have no conscious awareness. I think a prime example of this is when things come left of field or out of your awareness, and personally, I've found this often comes via a relationship – for example, getting work or a contract from someone somewhere down the line. What's interesting about this is that I would have expected most of my referral work to come from my close relationships;

surprisingly, it is frequently the relationships that are wider and outside my immediate network that provide me with the best contract work as they introduce a new relationship and then more work becomes available via a referral from the new contract. It links to the idea of not being able to connect the dots looking forward, but you can connect them looking back.

The key thing to recognise here is that when we are attached, we are in a state of fear rather than trust. We fear that if we don't achieve the outcome we desire, we will lose something – whether that's our self-worth, validation, or sense of who we are and our identity. This fear blocks the natural flow of energy and creativity. But the universe or god matter works in ways that are often beyond our immediate understanding. When we're too focused on controlling the "how" and "when" of things, we cut ourselves off from the endless possibilities that could bring about an even better result in a quicker timeframe. Attachment can blind us to these possibilities because we're so fixated on a single path to success.

Focus and illusion of control

When we are attached, we believe we can control the outcome through sheer determination. This illusion of control can cause frustration when things don't go according to plan. We become disheartened when the process doesn't move as quickly as we'd like or when obstacles arise. Our energy becomes stuck, and instead of allowing the natural flow of creation, we are constantly pushing against the current. I think you can still achieve results through determination; however, the speed and impact are reduced.

You commonly see this in business when launching a new project or business. If you're too attached to the business or project reaching a specific milestone or success within a tight timeframe, you might over-manage your team, push unnecessary deadlines, or make impulsive decisions based on fear. In your attachment, you hinder the project's natural growth and development.

On the other hand, when we are focused, this keeps us working diligently towards our goals but with an openness to different possibilities as to how it will unfold. Focus is about giving attention and energy to something, but without the emotional dependency on how or when it must evolve. Focus involves action and clarity, but leaves room for flexibility and unexpected outcomes. It enables you to act while staying connected to the bigger picture. It also creates space for creative solutions and new opportunities that may be even better than what you initially imagined.

Focus gives us clarity and direction without the desperation or neediness of attachment. It's the balance of intention and letting go – knowing that we're doing everything in our power to move towards our goals while trusting that the universe or god matter will take care of the details. We see this particularly in feminine flow, where we open ourselves up to experience the outcome being achieved in any way the universe or god matter sees fit. Remember, it is the end goal (chosen desired richness) or ultimate vision we are playing for. This is where we let the feminine energy of trust come in. You've taken action, and now you must trust that the results will unfold in divine timing. Just as you cannot rush the growth of a seed into a tree, you cannot rush the results of your aligned actions. Trust that the universe or god matter is working on your behalf to create whatever your heart desires.

This is where true magic happens, because it directs your energy without the emotional attachment to the result. When you are focused, you are present and proactive in taking steps towards your desired reality, but not obsessed with controlling how it shows up. We are still working towards a goal, but we are not becoming attached to any specific way in which it "has" to manifest. In business, this might mean launching the project, providing guidance and resources when necessary, and trusting your team and strategy to unfold as planned. You're still committed to driving the project forward, but you're not micro-managing every detail. You allow the process to develop with patience and trust in the systems and people in place.

Detachment: the key to freedom

Detaching from outcomes doesn't mean we stop caring or stop taking action. It simply means we release the need for things to happen a certain way. We trust that what's meant for us will unfold at the right time and in the right form. This means detaching from how that might look and be open to what unfolds. This allows us to stay grounded in the present moment, remain open to new opportunities, and adjust our course when necessary. It frees us from the emotional rollercoaster of needing things to go exactly as planned, which ultimately gives us more freedom and peace of mind.

When we combine focus with detachment, we unlock an incredible power. We stay dedicated to our goals, taking intentional action, but we're not rigid in how we expect the outcomes to appear. This flexibility is what leads to the greatest successes, because we allow the natural flow of life to bring us to exactly where we need to be.

The key takeaway here is that focus is essential for creation, but attachment often holds us back. The power of intention, combined with the ability to let go of specific outcomes, is a potent formula for creating our desires. When we are focused, we are clear about what we want and willing to take the necessary steps to get there. But when we're attached, we're stuck in a loop of needing things to happen in a certain way, which creates resistance and only one way for things to create themselves.

It's about staying committed to our vision while allowing the universe to fill in the details. It's about trusting that the right things will unfold at the right time and being open to how they show up. In the end, this balance is what brings peace and the ability to create from a place of freedom rather than fear.

21
Bringing into Being Through Action

Over the course of this book, we've explored the building blocks of creating your reality: understanding subconscious programming, the role of perception, balancing masculine and feminine energies, the power of belief, and the importance of focus. All these elements come together to understand that creation occurs from aligned action. This chapter is about moving from the theoretical, energetic, and mental aspects of creation into the tangible, physical results you can experience in life.

Throughout my life, I heard a lot about visualisation, but didn't see much about how to create which, for me, occurs through alignment of action. I often see that there is one crucial aspect which is overlooked, and that is taking action. It's not enough to visualise or to hold an intention. To bring something into your reality, you must act in alignment with your desires. You must take consistent, purposeful steps towards the outcome you want to create.

This doesn't mean frantic or forced action which is attached action. It means action that is inspired, focused, and guided by the inner knowledge you've developed through your vision and clarity, allowing the vision to get clearer and easier to see – so clear that it is already here in the present. The mistake many make is sitting on the couch and waiting for things to change, rather than stepping into their power and moving towards what they want, in the now, and taking the first steps to make the change happen now.

Visualisation as a starting point

Visualisation is an essential first step in creation, but it is not the full picture. Visualisation marks the moment when something not yet in your reality becomes a possibility in your mind. We have discussed this in earlier chapters – the importance of believing it can exist. It's about the potential or possibility. Nevertheless, just as planting a seed requires watering and care, visualisation must be followed by aligned action to bring it into reality.

My dad, for instance, had a powerful ability to visualise, but he would usually stop there. He would spend a lot of time visualising, sitting on the couch and seeing outcomes, but he didn't always follow up with the necessary actions to create. This was a bit of a family joke, but it served as a strong lesson for me: visualisation without action, in my view, is incomplete.

Earlier in the book, we discussed how subconscious programming shapes our reality and how our perception acts as a filter for what shows up in our lives. Here, we reinforce the idea that action plays a crucial role in reprogramming our subconscious mind. When we take aligned action, we start to gather new evidence, which shifts our belief systems. For example, if you've always believed that "nobody likes me", but you take action to put yourself out there and engage with others in social situations, you will start collecting evidence that challenges that belief. Each action chips away at the old programming, allowing new patterns to emerge. Your actions, therefore, help to rewire your subconscious mind.

We also explored the balance between masculine and feminine energies, with the masculine providing structure and the feminine allowing flow and creativity. Aligned action is the masculine energy that provides the structure for creation, while the feminine energy of inspiration and intuition guides that action. Think of it like this: the feminine energy generates the idea, the flow, vibrational alignment and the creative impulse. The masculine energy moves it forward into reality through action and structure. Both energies are essential. Without action, the idea remains just that: a possibility. Without feminine flow, the action becomes rigid, lacks creativity in how it will appear.

The role of belief and intention

In the chapter on belief, we explored how deeply held beliefs shape what's possible for us. Action is what reinforces this belief. Every time you take a step that aligns with your intention, you are telling yourself (and the network or universe and god matter) that you believe in the possibility of what you're creating, and this is where intention becomes critical. The power of your action is magnified when it is guided by clear, focused intention. If you are taking actions that are misaligned, you'll experience resistance, frustration, and lack of progress. But when your actions match the energy and vision of what you want to create, the results will flow.

The power of action

While visualisation sets the intention, action is what brings it forward. The key point here is that you must take aligned actions that are in harmony with the vision. The reason why I say "pulls it forward" is because it already exists. If we say push it forward, it means it doesn't exist yet.

You don't need to know the *how* behind your visualisation, but you do need to begin taking actions, even just small ones, to increase clarity. As you continue, each action refines your vision and clarifies what you need to do next. It's through the act of doing that you gain clarity and move closer to the result. For instance, in business, I've learned that trying to juggle multiple tasks simultaneously slows down progress. But when you focus on completing one task at a time, you move more quickly towards your desired outcome. You gain momentum. Each action you take refines the goal, and by continually refining and taking action, the result becomes inevitable.

Bringing into reality through action is about taking inspired, aligned steps towards your goal. It's about visualising, setting the intention, and then taking consistent actions that move you forward. Moreover, it's about being open to the flow, releasing rigid control, and allowing things to unfold in ways you may not have expected. Through this process, you not only achieve your goals but you also align with the deeper flow of creation, where the universe or god matter works with you to bring forth the reality you desire.

Think of it as stepping into the role of co-creator. You're no longer a passive observer of your reality. You are actively shaping it through your thoughts, beliefs, and most importantly, your actions. Every choice you make, and every step you take, is part of the creative process.

When we talk about taking action though, it's important to know that there are two parts to this. The first is just action, which in itself means doing things and taking steps that bring us closer to achieving our goals. The second, though, is inspired action, which comes from a place of higher energy or motivation. I personally don't think inspired action is divine guidance to take action. I think it comes from a place of higher frequency when taking an action. When you're aligned with your vision, you're more likely to feel inspired to take action. This higher frequency makes it easier to see what actions can be done and for us to take steps either towards it or in the opposite direction. Actions themselves are not right or wrong; rather, they're all just part of the journey to the outcome, and alignment is what influences the speed.

I just want to preface here that some actions are legally, morally and ethically wrong for the operation of society and community to work and I am not condoning the view of these actions to be seen as right or wrong. What I am saying is that every action becomes part of your journey and alignment to what you are creating; it creates the outcome you experience.

Practice as structure

Practice is the final piece of the puzzle here, whereby the practice is the structure or the routine that keeps you moving forward. This ties back to the masculine energy of structure and consistency. Your daily actions and habits create the framework through which your goals come to life. For example, by having a daily routine or habit that reinforces your intention, you're building the subconscious loop that moves you closer to your desired outcome.

It's essential to understand that bringing things into being isn't a one-time event. You take action, evaluate, refine, and take more action. Each step brings you closer to your goal.

Consistency is key in this. You may not see immediate results, but through persistent action, you plant seeds. These might not necessarily give you fruit, but they will still be of use and might provide you with other resources which you don't know you need right now. Sometimes, the harvest takes longer, but you know that it will come.

This was something my dad often struggled with, because although he would visualise, without consistent action the harvest was slow to come. However, even without understanding the full process, he managed to achieve results through his spiritual belief system which reinforced his trust that things would show up in his reality. He had pre-programmed his mind to expect certain outcomes, and because of that, they did eventually show up.

22

Mastering the Art of Being

Being is not just about existing; it's about how we vibrate, how we choose to show up, and how we embody the reality we wish to create. This concept goes beyond actions or thoughts. It's the totality of your unique presence; the essence of who you are at any given moment.

The power of choice in being

What's fascinating about being is that it's not static. It's constantly shifting, it's fluid, and we have a role in choosing how we show up every moment in every day. Every moment presents a choice to be something. You can be a person who reacts to anger, or you can be someone who chooses love. You can be a person who creates from a place of abundance, or you can be someone who reacts out of scarcity. The vibrational frequency you choose will determine the reality you create.

Choice is something that is always within our power. We choose to do things, and even when we don't act, we are still making a choice. This idea is often misunderstood, as even when we decide not to choose, we are creating outcomes through our inaction.

A great example of this is in relationships. You may choose not to speak up about a certain behaviour, and in your silence, you are effectively choosing to allow that behaviour to continue. It's only through communication that the other person can understand and decide whether to change their behaviour. If they don't, you still have the power to decide whether to stay or remove yourself from the situation.

I do want to acknowledge that there are circumstances where this approach may not be suitable – for example, in situations of extreme control or manipulation where communication and the ability to leave may be severely limited. But in most cases, our power lies in recognising the choices we are making, both in action and inaction, and understanding the impact they have.

The role of being in creation

As we have explored in previous chapters, action is required for creation, but it is the being that defines the nature of those actions. When we align our being with our intentions and focus, we can create anything we desire. Being isn't passive; it's an active, conscious state that guides how we move through life.

For example, if you want to create abundance in your life, you must *be* abundance. This means embodying the vibration of abundance before it even shows up in the physical world. It's about feeling, thinking, and acting as though what you desire is already here. This is the energetic foundation that supports the process of creation. However, there is a missing aspect in creating desired outcomes via vibration only. If someone were to truly take on a vibrational frequency that aligns with what they want to achieve, then in essence, it would already be here, simply in the time passage to be delivered. When you hold the vibration of an "I am" identity, you make choices aligned with the outcome, and each and every action and feeling is in alignment with the outcome being here. Nothing else can show up – it is already here, it is already done – as you are already the identity of the outcomes you seek. When your being has the belief and practice, the outcome is already available.

Being in the spiritual context

From a spiritual perspective, being is your essence – it's the unique vibrational frequency of your soul. When you are fully aligned with your true self, you are living in harmony with your divine purpose. You are not just reacting to the world; you are creating it from the inside out. Each one of us, although sharing common human experiences, has a unique distinct frequency shaped by our individual journey, the lessons we've encountered, and our unique blend of memories, beliefs, and emotions. This uniqueness makes our being deeply personal, yet there is also a commonality in the vibrational language of emotions that we all share.

Love, for instance, has a specific frequency that resonates similarly for everyone. It's a state of openness, expansion, and connection. Conversely, anger, although a frequency, is one that feels constricted, intense, and charged. Although our experiences of love or anger are deeply personal, the vibrational quality of these emotions is universal. When we realise this, we understand that our emotions carry energy that impacts not only our internal state but also the world we experience around us.

The key, then, is learning to consciously choose the frequency we embody moment to moment. By doing so, we start to take ownership of our vibrational state, influencing not just our inner experience but the way our external world shows up. You become the creator of your experience, shifting from a place of reaction to a place of intentional creation.

Further to this is the idea of "mirror, mirror" – reminiscent of the fairy tale line, "Mirror, mirror on the wall, who is the fairest of them all?" In this case, the mirror is the reflection of your inner self. The external world becomes a reflection of the internal world. It is your perception, beliefs, and emotions mirrored back to you. If your inner world is full of love, compassion, and acceptance, your external experiences will reflect those same qualities. The mirror you're looking into is not separate from you; it's your perception of reality bouncing back, confirming the frequency you're vibrating at. Mastering this mirror is where you focus on your internal being. When you change the way you are inside, your reality begins to transform, because what you see in the mirror is ultimately a reflection of your inner being.

By deliberately tuning into your higher energetic frequencies, you begin to manifest a reality that is more aligned with your true self and the essence of your soul's purpose. Thus, you become the creator of your life, consciously shaping your experience from the inside out.

Being versus doing

One important distinction to make here is the difference between being and doing, especially when we are consciously creating. In today's world, we regularly confuse the two and think they are the same thing. We think that doing more will lead to more success, more happiness, or more fulfilment. In reality though, being is the cause of all doing. If you are not in alignment with who you are being, all the actions you take will feel forced or out of sync, despite all of your hard work.

When we talk about creation through action, it's not about mindlessly doing things – it's about being the person who takes those actions. So often, people find themselves caught up in the doing – taking action simply for the sake of staying busy, without clear intention or direction. This kind of action can become a trap by keeping us in constant action, feeling busy but not necessarily moving us towards what we truly desire. The busyness fills the space, creating a sense of productivity that can distract us from the real essence of what we are trying to create. It becomes easy to mistake movement for progress, yet true creation starts with alignment – not just action.

Being, on the other hand, is something that is always present and evolving. It is not something we can turn on or off; it is the essence of who we are and the vibration we hold in every moment. Whether we realise it or not, we are always being something. The key lies in understanding that while being is a constant, the quality of our being – what frequency we vibrate at – can be consciously chosen. This choice of frequency is what defines the nature of our memories, our experience, and our ongoing reality. When we are in alignment, our being comes first, and the actions that follow are intentional, purposeful, and aligned with our highest vision. In this state, our doing is no longer just for the sake of staying busy; it is infused with meaning and directed towards a clear outcome.

Choosing the vibration at which we operate requires a level of awareness that is not always easy to maintain. It's about being conscious enough in each moment to decide how we want to be, even amidst daily challenges. The truth is, this isn't something I have mastered myself, especially not in every moment. There are times when I feel overwhelmed or living in frustration, anxiety, and fear, and I find myself reacting rather than consciously choosing my state of being. This is a continuous work in progress, a journey.

The process of mastering our being is deeply personal and continuous compassion for self. It's important to recognise that we expand through growth and awareness, and it's natural to have moments where we fall back into automatic reaction or unconscious subconscious behaviours. Each time we recognise that we have slipped into reaction, we gain an opportunity to realign and to consciously choose once more the frequency we want to embody, building an ability to recognise it quicker.

The idea of being versus doing also emphasises the difference between control and flow. Doing often comes from a desire to control – to force outcomes through sheer effort. Being, however, is about flow; it is about aligning with a higher vibrational frequency and allowing inspired action to emerge naturally from that alignment. When we are in a state of being, our actions are not forced – they are an extension of our aligned state, and they feel effortless because they are coming from a place of knowing, belief, and trust.

The challenge is to cultivate the awareness and mindfulness necessary to choose our state of being, even when circumstances around us seem chaotic. It is easy to fall into the trap of doing for the sake of doing, but true power lies in being, by first holding the vibration of what we wish to create, and then allowing our actions to flow naturally from that desired state. This is not to say that doing is unnecessary but rather that it should be the result of our being, not the other way around.

Ultimately, the journey is about learning to bring more awareness to our state of being and to intentionally align it with what we desire to create. It's about recognising when we are acting out of alignment and gently guiding ourselves back. It's about giving ourselves permission to pause, to breathe, and to choose our vibration consciously, even when the world seems to demand constant action. It's about finding the balance between effort and ease, and understanding that true creation comes from a place of inner alignment, rather than from continuous action without an ultimate desired outcome.

Being as the end of creation

Throughout this book, we have talked about the journey of creation and the role that beingness plays in pulling forth our desired reality. Being is both the beginning and the end of creation. It is the starting point from which everything flows and the culmination where all creation finds its true essence. Its "nature is in its nature", where something's true nature exists by virtue of itself, not because of anything external. Nothing else lies within and it is revealed by simply being what we are. In this sense, being is not a passive state; it is the core from which all action and desire emerges. At its deepest level, it is the very essence of who we are.

The concept of god matter plays a fundamental role in this process. God matter, or universal matter or the network, is the "being" in human being. It is the divine frequency that underlies everything we are and everything we create – it is all connected. Being is the origin, the process, and the destination; the emergence, the present, and the now; the opportunity, the understanding, and the knowing; the loss and the experience; the unwelcomed and the frightening. It is all of it. It is the essence that moves through all of existence, guiding your unfolding of your reality from one moment to the next.

From this perspective, god matter is the frequency – the vibrational energy that brings life into being, and the source of creation that exists within each of us. It is the beginning and the end, and everything in between. It is the force that connects us to all of it; to the divine, to the higher consciousness that exists beyond the limitations of our physical form. It is the spark within us that gives rise to our creativity, our desires, and our ability to bring ideas into reality.

In this way, we, as human beings, are the vessel – the machine that moves through the physical world – but it is god matter that is the program, the consciousness that drives us, our being. We are not just mechanical beings reacting to the world around us; we are conscious beings with the ability to consciously create our reality.

When we recognise that god matter is at the core of who we are, we understand that creation is not something that happens outside of us. It is something that emerges from within. The frequency of god matter within us is what determines our experiences and shapes our reality. By aligning with certain frequencies, we align ourselves with our desire, and we begin to create from a place of pure intention and divine connection.

The idea of being as both the beginning and the end means that creation is a cycle. It starts with being, pulls forth doing, and ultimately expands into a new form of being. It is a process of alignment, action, and creation that always leads us back to the core of who we are. When we are aligned with god matter or the universe, we become conscious creators, embodying the divine frequency and allowing it to guide our actions and shape our experiences.

We are not separate from the divine; we are an expression of it. And through our being, we become the bridge between the possible and the physical, bringing the frequency of god matter into form and creating a world that reflects our desire.

So, ask yourself: who are you being right now, and how is that shaping my reality?

Conclusion

Over the course of this book, we have been on a journey of beingness. We've journeyed through the depths of subconscious programming, how perception shapes our world, and the power of intention and focus in shaping our desired reality. Through this journey, the thread that ties everything together is the understanding that what you choose to believe, think, and embody becomes the essence of your lived reality.

We've also discussed the power of intention, the necessity of surrender, and the interplay between masculine and feminine energies. Each chapter invites you to not only think differently but to embody the changes as well, shifting your vibration to align with the life you truly desire. True creation does not happen in the hustle of endless doing; it manifests from a place of deliberate alignment, from choosing who you are being in every moment.

Throughout it all, the concept of "being" has been central to our discussion. Being is about more than just existing; it is about embracing a frequency that represents the essence of who you truly are and choose to be, in each moment. It is about stepping out of the habitual, reactionary loops that govern our lives and into conscious awareness. When you embrace your true being, your actions become a natural extension of your purpose. This shift – from forcing outcomes to allowing them – is where real magic happens. When you allow yourself to be, you create space for the universe to align in unexpected and miraculous ways.

Throughout the book, I have also invited you to challenge the beliefs and desires that have been ingrained by societal expectations. It's easy to be trapped in the cycle of wanting the next best thing – whether that's a bigger house, more money, greater achievements. But when we strip back the layers, we see that what we truly desire is often not the material object but the feeling we believe it will bring us – freedom, fulfilment, connection, and purpose. True wealth lies not in the things you possess, but in the richness of your experiences, the depth of your connections, and the freedom to choose how you spend your time.

By understanding and consciously shifting your identity, you create a ripple effect that touches every aspect of your life. Your relationships, business, and financial success are all reflections of who you are being. The changes we make on the inside reflect outward, influencing not only our own lives but also the lives of those around us. When we embody our true potential, we give others permission to do the same.

The journey from being the "created" to becoming the "creator" is one of empowerment. You are not a passive participant in your life. You have the power to shape your reality, to align with the highest version of yourself, and to manifest the vision that resonates with your soul.

As you move forward from here, remember that every moment is an opportunity to choose who you want to be. Your being is the foundation from which your actions arise. Surrender to the process, trust in the divine flow, and take inspired action to step into your true sense of being and pull forward your desired reality.

www.ingramcontent.com/pod-product-compliance
Lightning Source LLC
Chambersburg PA
CBHW040306170426
43194CB00022B/2918